KEYS TO RICHER LIVING

BOOKS BY DR. DUNNINGTON

Keys to Richer Living

Handles of Power

More Handles of Power

Start Where You Are

Something to Stand On

KEYS TO *Richer Living*

by Lewis L. Dunnington

THE MACMILLAN COMPANY

New York · 1952

FOREWORD

We live in a world of mounting tensions and uncertainty.

Having fought two world wars in a quarter of a century, the peace we fought for seems further away than ever. We are disillusioned. Millions of intelligent people seem to recognize no other values but money, physical comforts and material power. Unable to face up to the inevitable despair that such thinking generates, multitudes are employing the escape mechanism of alcohol. But always there comes the dreadful "morning after." Faster and faster grows the tempo of modern living as we try vainly to run away from reality.

But through all the chaos of these busy, hurrying days comes the still small voice of the Man of Galilee. He alone grows steadily in stature and in favor with God and man. He alone has the answers to our eternal quest for "peace at the center." In the pages that follow are certain basic and fundamental "Keys to Richer Living"—keys that if turned in the lock of life will open doors to lives of radiance, beauty and peace in spite of the confusions and bafflements of this troubled time.

In the preface to a previous book, *Something to Stand On,* we said that those chapters, delivered first as sermons in the Methodist Church in Iowa City, had built and held a large audience of 2,000, which necessitated two identical services each Sunday morning. The same remarkable response was had for the chapters of this book. Over half of this audience were students of all denominations who came in all kinds of weather.

Large numbers of private interviews with those of them who came to my study for counselling would seem to indicate clearly that the contents of the chapters that follow have helped to clarify their thinking and to furnish Keys to Richer Living.

My deep gratitude goes to Miss Evelyn Faucett, my secretary, for her typing and editing of the manuscript.

Lewis L. Dunnington

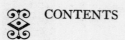 **CONTENTS**

THE BUNDLE OF LIFE

Body, Mind and Spirit make up the triangle of life. Anything that affects one leaves its imprint upon all, for body, mind and spirit constitute an interdependent whole. The statement that "we are what we eat" must be supplemented by "we are what we think" before we have the whole truth.

A chemical analysis of any human body will show that it is made up of the same elements to be found in any fertile acre of ground. This means that good earth and good bodies must contain potassium, phosphate and nitrogen plus about twenty of the so-called "trace elements." Plants can take only what the earth contains and the human body can receive only what the plant has received from the soil. Poor soil means, therefore, devitalized bodies, which in turn infers crooked thinking and wrong living with its attendant unhappiness and frustration. How eternally true was the statement of the author of I Samuel (25:29): *"The soul of my lord shall be bound in the bundle of life with the Lord thy God."*

Take that experiment performed some time ago in a hospital in Birmingham, Alabama. Six healthy, normal women were given everything they wanted to eat except that a trace of thiamin (Vitamin B-1) was taken from their diet. They progressively deteriorated in body, mind and spirit until at the end of a month they were depressed and despondent, unable to eat or sleep or think. Then thiamin was restored to their diet and in another month they were as well as ever and enjoying life to the full. Let us admit at once that God could not answer those women's prayers for health of body and mind until they lived up to the laws of his universe and started eating the right kind of food. *We are bound in the bundle of life with the Lord our God.*

The United States contains a hundred and fifty million of the best-fed people on earth and yet we are slowly dying of starvation! Hay fever has doubled in twenty-five years, heart disease has increased sixty per cent in twenty years. Arthritis and cancer are increasingly attacking millions of people every year. These so-called degenerative diseases have baffled the entire medical fraternity, but new light is beginning to dawn. It is now believed that they are intimately allied with the progressive deterioration of the soil and that we shall never be a healthy people until we use our intelligence to restore our impoverished ground.

Recently I toured the TVA region and was thrilled at what I saw. Fifteen short years of applied intelligence has done more for the four million inhabitants of that region than has ever been done in a comparable situation in the history of the world.

Briefly the story runs as follows: The inhabitants removed the top covering of trees and sod and cropped the land for several generations without putting anything back into the soil. Fifty inches of rainfall a year continued to wash and bleed the rolling land until little but subsoil was left. People and animals were slowly starving to death. The degenerative diseases progressively took their awful toll while crime and juvenile delinquency flourished.

Then came the TVA and a miracle. Twenty-six dams were built to control the water and generate vast power. The huge deposits of phosphate rock at Muscle Shoals were ground up and put back into the land. Alfalfa and clover were grown and turned under for humus. Scrawny, diseased cattle and hogs began to look better and better as did the people. Crime and juvenile delinquency began to decrease as human bodies began to be rebuilt. Income from rebuilt land began to double and treble as hope returned. New schools and churches are replacing old dilapidated structures as the miracle of the TVA continues to unfold. One farmer told us as we stood looking at a beautiful field of corn: "I used to get half a wagon load of corn nubbins from that field but last year I got sixty bushels of excellent corn to the acre."

The inhabitants of the Tennessee valley are very religious and I saw churches everywhere. But to pray for health and the good life until they were helped to rebuild their impoverished soil but revealed their ignorance of the laws of an orderly universe. Such praying reminds one of the bus driver in the Himalayas. He was about to start over one of the most dangerous and winding roads in the world. So he walked around in front of his engine and stood with folded hands, praying for a successful trip. An hour out on the road and his engine overheated with a boiling radiator. He had neglected to fill it before starting. Halfway up the steepest grade of the trip, he burned out a bearing. He had forgotten to check his oil level. A prayer to God for quiet courage and stamina in the face of dangerous driving conditions could be answered. But when the driver left the oil and water business to God also instead of using his own intelligence, *God could do nothing but let him learn his lesson!*

Louis Bromfield is devoting his life to a missionary crusade to awaken his fellow-countrymen to these very truths. He tells us that two heads of lettuce that look alike may vary up to seventy-five per cent in mineral content, depending on the contents of the soils in which they grew. The nutritive value to the eaters of those heads of lettuce would vary accordingly. The time is not far distant when produce grown on certified farms of standard soil richness will command much higher prices than produce not so certified.

I recently read an article by Dr. J. A. Shield in the *Journal of the Southern Medical Association* entitled "Farm Practices Influencing the Incidence of Multiple Sclerosis." He writes that this rapidly increasing plague is a degenerative disease undoubtedly caused by diet that is deficient in some of the trace elements—iron, cobalt, copper, boron, zinc chlorine, sodium, magnesium, manganese and sulphur.

A deficiency in any one of these trace elements can cause serious trouble. In New Zealand great numbers of sheep were becoming paralyzed. An examination of the soil on which the grass grew showed a deficiency in cobalt. When a little of this mineral was added to the soil the paralysis disappeared.

Down in Florida the orange trees were developing mottle-leaf. When a tiny bit of zinc oxide was put into the soil near each tree the mottle-leaf disappeared. Around Mt. Chocorua in New Hampshire, farmers found it impossible to raise cattle. They always died and many people believed the old legend that an Indian chief had once put a curse on the white man's stock. However, when agricultural experts discovered a complete absence of barium in the soil and remedied that defect, the cattle began to thrive.

Time magazine for September 19, 1949, gives us more food for thought along this line. It tells us there is a "goiter belt" running from Western New York through the Great Lakes basin and across the plains to the Rockies, caused by the lack of a tiny bit of iodine in the diet. Dr. William H. Sebrell of "Public Health Services" is quoted as saying that this lack of iodine in the diet may and often does result in lowered efficiency and nervousness for an entire lifetime. A tiny bit of iodine put into "Iodized salt" takes care of the situation. The thyroid gland takes up iodine from the blood stream and uses it to form a hormone, thyroxine. In turn thyroxine regulates many bodily functions, including heat production, brain development, sexual maturity, and growth of hair, skin and bones.

Think about that for a moment—our brain development, sexual maturity and the growth of healthy hair, skin and bones is dependent on having a trace of iodine in the diet! Yet we are told that only about one third of the salt sold in the iodine deficient region of the Middle West is "iodized salt" for the reason that many housewives suspect such salt is "medicated"! Of course it is! And without it their families can never be perfectly well!

Even when our food comes from good land, we often ruin it in the process of preparing it for the table. When the water in which vegetables are boiled is poured down the sink a large part of the minerals for which our bodies cry out is thrown away. Modern Home Economics courses teach that very little water should be used and that little should be later served with the vegetable.

Volumes have been written about the crime of making white flour by throwing away the bran which contains chemical elements absolutely essential to bodily well-being. Up until recently, the average loaf of white bread may have tasted good but it really was not fit for a hog to eat. In fact, the average hog would die on a white-bread diet. Millers have recently started enriching the bread by the addition of certain vitamins.

The great importance of all we have been trying to say becomes clearly apparent when we read Dr. Edward Spencer Cowles' challenging book "Don't Be Afraid." Dr. Cowles is Director of the Park Avenue Hospital, New York, and Staff Physician and Psychologist to the Bloodgood Foundation of Johns Hopkins University. He has successfully treated many, many thousands of people suffering from worry, fear, frustration and failure.

The thesis of this book, studded with case histories, is that *the basis of most fear is FATIGUE which in turn is caused by malnutrition*. Malnutrition is caused by eating devitalized food or by worrying so much that the food we do eat upsets the digestive system and fails to give nourishment. Body and mind are thus interdependent—bound together in the bundle of life.

Dr. Cowles has an all-important chapter on "Measuring Nerve Cell Energy." Taking 100 units of nerve cell energy as norm for a perfectly well individual with abundant health, he shows us that we have a safety margin of nerve energy between 80 and 100 units upon which we may draw without ill effects. There are thus times when we may overwork, neglect our diet, worry over this or that and still be in no danger of developing a psychoneurosis. But "once your nerve cell energy drops below 80 units and nothing is done to send it up again, you are in the neurotic field whether you like it or not." When nerve cell energy drops below 60 units one is in the melancholia field and in great danger.

There is thus a "psychic threshold" of health represented by 80 units. *When our supply of nerve energy drops below that point, the fears, worries and frustration normally buried in the deep or unconscious mind break over into the conscious mind and we are mentally ill.* Then, as the fatigue state of the nerve cells progresses, impulses break over the psychic threshold with increased force until such time as the energy level is built up again.

Dr. Cowles has proved over and over again in his Body and Mind Clinic that depression, fear, terror and irritability are caused by fatigue and that his first duty to the patient is to rebuild his store of nervous energy. Then he is able successfully to treat the mind and to bring the patient back to health and a normal outlook on life, devoid of fear and worry.

The importance of what and how we eat, therefore, cannot be exaggerated. "We are what we eat" and "We are what we think." But, being bound together in the bundle of life with the Lord our God, these two statements go together and suggest complete interdependence. Every person who hopes to be well and happy is obligated to make a careful study of his diet. With a doctor's advice he would probably do well to supplement his diet with vitamin tablets. He would be wise to drink lots of water, exercise daily in the fresh air and get plenty of rest. Dr. Cowles has proved that the average person can be perfectly well if he wishes to be.

The conclusion of the matter then is simply this: Man is a strange and wonderful unity of body, mind and spirit. A healthy mind and spirit are dependent on a sturdy body because we are "bound together in the Bundle of Life." But a healthy body is a wonderful chemical laboratory which must keep on drawing its basic elements steadily from food raised on fertile soil. Washed out and depleted soils cannot give to food that which they do not have. Hence the crying need for intelligence in our whole agricultural program if we would coöperate with God in building sturdy bodies that in turn can house healthy minds and spirits.

It is quite possible that some reader may be asking, "Why doesn't the author write about religion and leave the question of diet to the dietitians?" To which we must reply that "If this is not a subject of extraordinary religious importance then we wouldn't know what to call it!" We are bound together in the bundle of life *with the Lord our God*. Because of the interdependent way he has created us, he is helpless to answer our prayers for good health until we use our intelligence in obeying his laws.

THE RAW MATERIAL OF LIFE

We have all heard the story of how Michelangelo took a huge block of marble on which another sculptor had labored without success some forty years earlier, and produced the colossal and justly famous statue of David. As one looks upon this great masterpiece in the city of Florence, he is bound to reflect upon the fact that two men may be given the same raw materials with which to work but one will fail while the other gloriously succeeds. Why? The answer to that question lies buried deep within the personalities of the artists themselves and not in the raw materials with which they work.

We are all given pretty much the same raw materials of life. Some succeed, others fail. It depends on the attitude we bring to them. Some say fickle chance or lady luck is the deciding factor and chance would indeed seem to play its part. But even when chance has thrown up this or that unexpected circumstance, the final outcome will be determined by what we do with it.

In G. Lynn Summer's book, *Meet Abraham Lincoln,* the author says chance made Abraham Lincoln president. Chance certainly played its part but what Lincoln did with the stray pieces of this puzzle of life finally determined the outcome. An invitation came to Lincoln in 1859 to deliver a lecture in Plymouth Church in Brooklyn for two hundred dollars. Our poor Springfield lawyer needed the money. About this time word came that son Robert had failed in fifteen out of sixteen entrance examination subjects as he sought admission to Harvard. Verily he needed his father's advice and encouragement.

This decided the matter and Lincoln started east. The lecture was shifted to Cooper Union to accommodate more people and Lincoln "held the vast meeting spellbound by his logic, and at the close, the audience broke into wild and prolonged enthusiasm." We are bound to note right here that it was what our gaunt friend brought to that chance lecture that turned the trick. It brought him the opportunity to make eleven other speeches on his way to see his son Robert.

From that time on he was a presidential candidate albeit a second-rater. Up until the very night of the vote in the Republican convention hall in Chicago, William H. Seward seemed destined to win by an overwhelming majority. But the tally sheets which an unreliable printer failed to deliver that night on schedule held the final vote up until the next day, giving Lincoln's followers an extra night of feverish work among the delegates. That turned the tide. Even there, however, it was what Lincoln had done with his life that gave his workers their arguments and not least among them were some of the actual rails that he had split as a young man, marking him as a hard-working pioneer. It was more than chance that made Lincoln president.

Look at what he did, for example, with a bit of raw material years before. He had been a Whig all his life but found he could not effectively fight slavery from within the party. When the infant Republican party was forming he was warned not to jeopardize his future by associating with those radical nobodies. He went to a Bloomington meeting anyway and was called upon for a speech. "At first he spoke slowly and haltingly, but gradually he grew in force and intensity until his hearers arose from their chairs and with pale and quivering lips pressed unconsciously toward him. Starting from the back of the broad platform on which he stood, his hands on his hips, he slowly advanced toward the front, his eyes blazing, his face white with passion, his voice resonant with the force of his conviction. . . . He seemed like a giant inspired." Reporters present forgot to take notes as they joined the cheering, stamping throng but they agreed that Lincoln welded that discordant and incongruous assembly into a group that came to feel as one man.

Sometimes chance hands an individual the rawest possible kind of a deal and then it is strictly up to the afflicted one to sink or swim, survive or perish. During the war a young Australian was hit by a piece of shrapnel and lost his right arm. For a time he lay unconscious on the field. Then two stretcher-bearers saw him move and went out to carry him back. A shell burst near by killing both bearers and taking off both of the Australian's legs. When he was finally rescued and nursed back to life, he seemed indeed to have reached the dead end of a blind alley. After all, what could a man do with no legs and only one arm?

Yet today that boy is one of the most successful automobile salesmen in Australia. He was fitted with artificial limbs at a hospital in England and given rehabilitation training. Then, with faith in God and mankind and in himself he began the steady climb toward self-support and the complete readjustment to the world that his handicap required. The raw material for the comeback looked formidable enough. But what he did with it was of supreme importance to himself and to all other handicapped veterans.

Perhaps someone is saying to himself, "Yes, I even think that I might take a very bad situation and do something fine with it—there would be such a challenge for each hour and plenty of encouragement from admiring friends. But the dull routine monotony of the average life where nothing ever happens finally gets one down. What can one do with such raw material?"

That is what a boy like Frederick Greenleaf might have thought at one time. Born in 1820 in a small town in Maine, Frederick faced the same humdrum daily grind that most people do. For a few years before his death he was the manager of the Worcester freight office of the old Boston and Worcester Railroad. He was a very cheerful person and made a point every day of easing as much of the burden of common people as possible by doing many little acts of kindness for them.

Edward Everett Hale who was then a young minister in a Unitarian

Church in Worcester, was deeply impressed by the young man's unfailing kindness and goodwill. For thirty years he carried Frederick Greenleaf's memory with him until he wrote it into a story called "Ten Times One Is Ten." The idea of the story is that an habitually kindly person unconsciously inspires all the individuals who come in touch with him and that if practical helpfulness can thus be spread by enough people, the whole world will finally be converted to the religion of Faith and Hope and Love.

In writing the story Edward Everett Hale suggested four mottoes for daily living:

> Look up and not down,
> Forward and not back,
> Out and not in
> And lend a hand!

The story took America by storm and countless numbers of societies were formed with the avowed intention of spreading practical kindness —Lend-A-Hand Clubs, Ten-Times-One Clubs, Look-Up Legions and others. Thus the record of simple kindness of an insignificant freight agent became the means of helpfulness to thousands and even millions of a later generation he was never to see.

Take another look at Hale's mottoes—Look up, not down; forward and not back; out, not in—and lend a hand. That is sound psychology. It enables us to turn the stream of consciousness away from self toward God and man thus making extroverts of us. We thus have no time for the introversion that may cause worry, frustration and fear. And by lending a hand we make others happy and, as bread cast upon the water returns after many days, we too find real happiness through a strange law of indirection. The raw materials may not be glamorous, but they turn out to contain a potent magic when properly manipulated.

At other times the materials for life transformation may be mysteriously tied in with a few simple words of challenge thrown out by some person at a moment of deep and haunting need in some listener. This happened to William H. Danforth. As a lad he was a sickly, sallow-cheeked, hollow-chested boy who envied the more tough, robust children in his school.

One day a teacher who was a health crank spoke vigorously on the theme of developing a strong body and, seeming to look directly at

Willie Danforth, he said with flashing eyes: "I dare you to fill your body with fresh air, wholesome food, and faithfully to exercise every day until your cheeks are rosy, your chest full and your limbs sturdy."

Danforth says that by this time his blood was up and his decision made. The dare gripped him and he went to work. "Today," he adds, "just sixty-two years later, there are only two of that class of fifty-two boys living and the sickest boy of all is one of them." William H. Danforth not only became physically strong but he made a fortune selling Purina products and then established a Foundation for distributing the money in the wisest way for the benefit of other human beings. He wrote a book called, *I Dare You,* which I have read with profit and which he gives to high schools and Y.M.C.A.'s to be put into the hands of boys and girls who need to be challenged to start climbing where they are.

Sometimes one hears students in a great university giving voice to pessimistic views about their future hopes. They wish they had been born in the good old days when a young man had a chance to make something of his life! Reminds me of the speech of the United States Commissioner of Labor in 1886 when he said: "The next fifty years (1886 to 1936) will probably show no such advances, no such opportunities for ambitious individuals as the last fifty years (1836 to 1886). The day of large profits in business and industry is now (1886) probably past."

Yes, sir, those were his gloomy predictions for the fifty years from 1886 to 1936. But what happened? The electric light, telephone, automobile, motion picture, airplane, radio, electric refrigerator, oil furnace, and air conditioning units were all invented during that half century, thus causing the greatest industrial revolution of all time. Those inventions were developed by men who looked up, not down; forward, not back; out, not in; and who lent a hand!

Good friends, the raw materials for the good life are all around us in rich abundance. Some of them look tough and unpromising, but they all contain almost limitless possibilities. It all depends on what we determine to do with them. Problems of ill health, financial difficulty, discordant human relations, boredom or unhappiness can be met and mastered if we believe they can.

> If you think you are beaten, you are.
> If you think you dare not, you don't.

> If you'd like to win but are sure you can't,
> It's almost certain you won't.
> First prizes don't always go
> To the brightest and strongest man:
> Again and again the one who wins
> Is the one who is sure that he can.

COMING TO TERMS WITH LIFE

When Margaret Fuller told Carlyle she had accepted the universe and he replied, "Gad you'd better," they were giving evidence of a profound insight into life. Millions of neurotic people are ill and unhappy and caught in a veritable prison house of negativity because they steadfastly refuse to accept the universe. They center their rebellious minds on the evil that frustrates them and thereby intensify its malevolent hold.

William James used to say, "Be willing to have it so. Acceptance of what has happened is the first step in overcoming the consequence of any misfortune." He was merely saying that such acceptance frees the mind from agitated resistance in order that it may be centered on the positive, healing approach to the difficulty. The most serious form of mental fixation or melancholia results from an imprisonment of the spirit that is in ceaseless conflict with the decrees of unhappy circumstance. That is the meaning of the old Negro spiritual: "You can't get over it, you can't get around it, you can't get under it, you must come in at the door." It is the deep wisdom of Jesus' teaching not to resist evil. "Ye have heard that it hath been said, Thou shalt love thy neighbor and hate thine enemy. But I say unto you, Love your enemies, bless them that curse you, do good to them that hate you, and pray for them that despitefully use you and persecute you. That ye may be the children of your Father which is in heaven."

This is no weak-kneed doctrine for the impotent. It is in line with the best modern psychology and utterly indispensable if our maladjustment and disease is to eventuate in health, wholeness and happiness. Love must come to dominate as the principle which enables us to overcome evil with good. Health is not merely the absence of disease, and emotional adjustment does not inevitably follow a clearing of the mind of negative fixations. The vacuum must be filled with the positive life-giving attitudes. If we would be psychically well, there must be a more potent factor present than the mere absence of enmity and bitterness. We must first accept the evil condition and then center the mind on the Love, Truth and Goodness of God as the one, all-inclusive, healing principle of life.

When Thomas Carlyle had finished writing *The French Revolution* he took the huge manuscript to his neighbor, John Stuart Mill. After some days, Mill appeared at Carlyle's door one morning. He was white as a sheet and completely unnerved. The maid had used it to start a fire.

For days Carlyle raged like a mad man. Two years of the hardest work of his life had gone up in smoke. He thought he could never write again. But one morning as he stood mournfully looking off across the roof tops near his home, he saw a stone mason building a house. Slowly, patiently, he observed the man laying on brick as the wall gradually took form.

With that vision came *acceptance* of his frustration and the dawn of the realization that he too could rewrite his book page by page. His mind at rest, he set to work again and gave the world, at long last, what is said to be his finest work—the colossal compilation of the story of the French Revolution.

A good illustration of the change that takes place in any life when the mind is shifted from the negative to the positive approach is found in the memoirs of D. L. Moody. Once when he was holding meetings in St. Louis he preached on the Philippian jailer. The next morning the local paper covered the meeting under the rather sensational heading, "How the Jailer of Philippi Was Caught."

A notorious criminal by the name of Valentine Burke sat in his cell and idly gazed at the headline. He had once been in Philippi, Illinois, and supposed the story related to the jailer in that town. Wishing to see how the jailer was caught he read the story from Paul as Moody told it. Puzzled he looked at the date on the paper on the masthead thinking it must be an old paper. Since it was dated that morning the mystery was as deep as ever.

As he thrust the paper aside in disgust Moody's text kept recurring to him: "Believe on the Lord Jesus Christ and thou shalt be saved." Moody used it nine times in that one sermon. Finally at midnight

Valentine Burke prayed for the first time in his life and, in faith, accepted the forgiveness of God that released him from his fear and hatred of jailers and all other men.

The sequel is most interesting. On his release from prison, the warden had him shadowed. After all, he was a notorious repeater in the world of crime and this religion stuff must be a blind. Burke went to New York City and sought honest employment, frankly telling everybody he was a jailbird with a bad record who now intended going straight. Nobody believed him and he remained unemployed and finally drifted back to St. Louis.

One day the warden sent for him and asked him what he had been doing since his release. Burke told his story. "You are exactly right," said the warden. "I have had you shadowed for I did not believe you really intended to go straight. Your story coincides in every detail with what my detective has told me of your life since leaving St. Louis. I need another deputy and I'm offering you the job."

Burke gladly took the position and spent the rest of his life there as a trusted employee. In his conversion experience he ceased to rage against the whole world of mankind *when he accepted the fact that his way of life was dead wrong* even to the point of continuing to tell prospective employers how wrong he had been. But of far greater importance than that was his repeated insistence that God had forgiven him and put his feet on the straight and narrow path. This was the new center of life on which his whole mind and heart was centered and which brought him the unbelievable dividends of peace and success.

I recently called on a remarkable young woman in the hospital. The thermometer stood at exactly 100 degrees and the humidity registered 80 degrees. The first two people I visited were perspiring and miserable. They complained bitterly about the weather. But when I reached the bedside of the young lady in question, I found her serene and smiling in spite of the fact that she had been in a cast for several months.

In response to my remark that it was a joy to find someone feeling so cheerful on such a blistering, hot day she said: "You don't mind the heat if you accept it as a part of the inevitable. When I first fell and the doctor feared my injury was irreparable, I surrendered to the inevitable and found it much easier to bear. Now, by the help of

God, I am surprising the doctor by making steady progress toward eventual health. The first thing we have to do is to accept the inevitable and go on from there."

This same principle has been demonstrated thousands of times in the long history of mankind. After wandering around in the desert for forty years Moses became impatient to take his people into the Promised Land. So he sent twelve spies up there to look around and bring back a report.

All twelve saw precisely the same difficulties—the giant and ferocious character of the inhabitants and the incredible richness of the land flowing with milk and honey. Ten of the spies "accepted" the situation without faith that the land could be taken. It "is a land that eateth up the inhabitants thereof: and all the people that we saw in it are men of great stature," they said. Then came the revealing conclusion: "We were in our own sight as grasshoppers, and so we were in their sight." Notice that sequence. They were as grasshoppers in their own sight and therefore they concluded they must look that way to the inhabitants and that meant the taking of the land should not even be considered.

But how different was the report of Caleb and Joshua! They too accepted the situation for what it was—difficult. "Let us go up at once and possess it; for we are well able to overcome it." Here was faith and confidence in abundance without which no enterprise can possibly succeed.

The fearful counsel of the ten, however, was accepted by the people and they thereby doomed themselves to wander another forty years in the desert. When at long last the children of Israel did go up to take the land, Caleb and Joshua were the only ones left who passed over Jordan with the triumphant invaders. All of the rest had died, defeated by their own negative attitude. Listen to Caleb as he went on into the Promised Land: "I am this day as I was the day that Moses sent me, as my strength was then, even so is my strength now."

One of the basic facts of life that we all need to face with clear minds before the day of trouble dawns is the truth contained in a rugged passage in Ecclesiastes 9:2: "All things come alike to all: There is one event to the righteous and to the wicked; to the good and to the clean and to the unclean; to him that sacrificeth, and to him that sacrificeth not: . . ." The writer of these words is not here referring to evil that men bring on themselves through ignorance, folly and sin. He is saying that epidemics, earthquakes, automobile and airplane accidents and many other natural evils are just as apt to afflict a good man as a bad.

One of the questions every minister hears oftener than any other is, after such a calamity has fallen: "What have I done that this should happen to me?" The answer is, my friend, that you haven't done anything. Eventually, in this realm of "natural evil," "all things come alike to all," and you would do well to accept that fact before the blow falls instead of thinking God has something against you.

Through this simple act of acceptance you are then ready to pray for strength and courage to start where you are and go on from there. And God can and will answer that prayer as he did for Jesus. Please bear in mind that Jesus tried to escape from the awful calamity of the cross even at the eleventh hour. He prayed that that fearful cup might pass from him. He was blameless. He had done nothing to deserve the death that loomed ahead. Then he accepted the situation: "Nevertheless not my will but thine be done," and God then gave him the fortitude and courage to carry on to the bitter end.

Even when our fear has brought us woe we still need the principle of acceptance. I am thinking at the moment of the millions of people who stutter and who suffer unspeakable anguish daily in their struggle to talk without getting into the emotional jam that ties them up.

I talked to a man recently who has almost freed himself from this dreadful condition during the last six months. For twenty years, since he was three or four years old, he had stuttered. Fear of stuttering had kept him a prisoner all that time. He avoided consonants when he could. He avoided people and resorted to a sign language whenever possible.

Then through a friend's advice he accepted the situation. He learned to relax with faith in God and in himself. With this new attitude he deliberately and joyously sought people out and started to talk to them. Observing that he had stuttered worse at the end of the day when he was physically tired, he began to pay strict attention to the laws of health and to take a long nap at noon so that he was always physically at his best.

He said to me: "It worked miraculously. My stuttering dropped away with my fear and my fatigue. If I blocked up on the word 'break,' I tossed it at the next person I met with joyous anticipation. My conquest became an exciting game and as the weeks wore on and I steadily improved I knew I had won."

These are the principles advocated by Wendell Johnson, able director of the Speech Clinic here at the University of Iowa. Mr. Johnson himself is the shining example for the young people in the clinic, for he has conquered the demon that held him captive for years. He helps eliminate their fear by demonstrating daily that stuttering *can* be overcome.

"Give us, O give us, the man who sings at his work," said Carlyle. "He will do more in the same time and he will do it better than the sullen individual." The singing man has accepted the situation for the moment, until he can find his way to the completion of his task or until he can find something better.

Here we should insert a word of caution to our young friends to avoid confusing shyness with fear. They are not the same at all. It is discreditable, under the age of twenty-five, not to be shy. Too much self-assurance in the very young indicates a lack of sensibility and the boy or girl who is not shy at twenty will probably be a bore at forty. For shyness is a God-given protective shield behind which our personalities are able to develop. Shyness may seem inconvenient at times but a reasonable amount of it will be a blessing *if it is accepted as such.*

That is where faith must play its vital role. Acceptance and faith belong together in the age-long struggle with doubt and frustration.

And what is faith? The anchored trust that at the core of things
Health, goodness, animating strength flow from exhaustless springs;
That no star rolls unguided down the rings of endless maze,
That no feet tread an aimless path through wastes of empty days;
That trusts the everlasting voice, the glad, calm voice that saith
That Order grows from Chaos, and that life is born from death;
That from the wreck of rending stars behind the storm and scathe,
There dwells a heart of central calm;—and this, and this is faith.[1]

[1] From "The Higher Catechism" by Sam Walter Foss. Lothrop, Lee & Shepard Co. Inc. Used by permission.

BASIC ASSUMPTIONS

Life is a continuous adventure into the unknown. Each new day is an hitherto unlived experience wherein we begin a tour of exploration where no man's foot has ever trod. To go to school, to make friends, to go into business, to fall in love, to marry, to rear children, to walk confidently into a future which no one can predict for so much as one hour is a thrilling adventure to the man of faith.

This unknown road of life is constantly forking. One branch leads this way and another that, necessitating a series of important decisions. We cannot stand still, for the tide of life moves inexorably on with every tick of the clock. We must decide—but how? *That all depends on what our habitual assumptions are.* George Bernard Shaw has said: "What a man believes may be ascertained not from his creed, but from the assumptions on which he habitually acts." Those assumptions, in turn, will depend on what we have faith in. "It is faith in something," as Oliver Wendell Holmes put it, "which makes life worth living," and, he might have added, that determines which fork of the road we shall decide to take.

Do we believe that there is a God who is "Our Father"? That he knows us individually and cares more than we can ever know what happens to us? That he has created a universe that is essentially friendly? Do we believe that the universe is shot through and through with the majestic and irrevocable demands of the Moral Law? That the ultimate values all have to do with the infinite worth of every human soul? That Christ is earth's most perfect revelation of God?

If our answer to these queries be a ringing affirmative, our habitual assumptions will be so based. No fork in life's road will halt us for long. If our answers, however, should be in the negative, our ultimate decisions will be entirely changed and our lives will unfold under a decidedly different pattern.

If we think there is *no* God, no friendly universe, no Moral Law and no future life, that also is faith; that also is belief. It is a basic assumption without hope and without incentive to noble living. Many an honest and sincere young life is beclouded by doubt during the early years of rather natural revolt against some of the traditional beliefs of childhood. I was brought up to believe in a God with a body like a man, with a long flowing, white beard and seated on a golden throne. I believed in a heaven with pearly gates and golden streets and in a hell of literal brimstone fires. I believed in a verbally inspired Bible which taught that the earth was made in six days of twenty-four hours each.

When certain college courses forced me to revise and reinterpret these childhood conceptions I was in a dither of uncertainty. I was fortunate enough to be able to keep one fixed point of reference— an unshakable belief in a good and loving God. I became an agnostic about other beliefs, frankly admitting that I did not know. Tolstoi once said, after a period of storm and stress: "I remembered that I only *lived* at those times when I believed in God." I clung to that with the desperation of a drowning man and finally, after years of open-minded search after God's own truth, came through to a sane, intellectually and emotionally satisfying faith.

George Eliot never came through. Just at the age when her mind was waking to independent thought she came into possession of Hennell's *Inquiry Concerning the Origin of Christianity*. No one was at hand to interpret constructively the questions raised by the devastating arguments in his book. She became lost in a fog of doubt and never recovered her faith. Dr. F. W. H. Meyers later told of walking with her in a garden at Cambridge on a rainy evening in May. With terrible earnestness she stated that a belief in God was inconceivable, that immortality was unbelievable and that only duty remained absolute and peremptory. Duty, however, unaided by faith in God and immortality, would prove a weak and unstable reed on which to lean.

Robert Browning fared better. He had his period of revolt and questioning and, in his sixteenth year, was even rebuked in church for "intentional misbehavior." He had read Shelley's "Queen Mab" and straightway declared himself an atheist! But in his *Pauline*, written in his twenty-first year, he speaks of "a need, a trust, a yearning after God" and we know that he was well on his way toward one of the most robust and vital of Christian faiths. As he looked back upon his period of early doubt from the high vantage point of a secure refuge in God and in a moral universe, he called his early revolt "the passionate, impatient struggles of a boy toward truth and love."

This period of uncertainty became an element of strength to the poet who ultimately became "the friend and aider of those who would live in the spirit." His basic and habitual assumptions were God-centered. In "Fra Lippo Lippi" he cries:

> This world's no blot for us,
> Nor blank; it means intensely, and means good:
> To find its meaning is my meat and drink.

As Dr. Edwin Mims says: "In his poetry all the discords of his age are harmonized. In this novel, quick, variegated world, he was 'aware of a central peace where the noise was quieted and the tangle unraveled.' "[1]

Faith in God gives frustrated, beaten, suffering man his securest refuge and his greatest source of recuperative power. When one of our church boys came home from months of incarceration in a German prison camp, he told us that daily prayer meetings were a constant source of comfort and strength. Some of the boys didn't know many hymns, but those they did know were sung with gusto and power. "You should have heard them go to town with 'The Church in the Wildwood,' " he said. They had no hymnals and some boy would recall a verse of something like "My Faith Looks Up to Thee" and would write it down on wrapping paper so that other boys could use it as copy. After a songfest "it was touching to see how carefully each boy folded his 'hymn book' and tucked it in his billfold."

How many families there are in every parish where some member is desperately ill and where their prayers rise night and day like a fountain. It is then that the minister comes to realize that what is needed most of all is not to know the explanation, but to know *that there is an explanation;* to possess the faith that somehow, somewhere beyond the stars the meaning will come clear.

Thomas Carlyle weathered a spiritual revolution in his own life and then, having found his own soul, set out to goad other men to

[1] *Great Writers as Interpreters of Religion* by Edwin Mims, p. 169. Abingdon-Cokesbury Press. Used by permission.

find theirs. It was in 1819 that he was struggling with the spiritual crisis recorded in *Sartor Resartus*. By 1837 when his famed *French Revolution* appeared, he was a veritable one-man typhoon out to sweep away man's inhumanity to man from the face of the earth. Through its moulten lines, written at white heat, peer the faces of France's poverty-stricken masses, "prowling through all the highways and byways of French existence." "Emptiness of pocket, of stomach, of head, and of heart," finally goaded these "uncomforted, untaught, and unfed" multitudes until they tore the lid off the seething cauldron that was France.

"The cause of this suffering and of the revolution is found in the selfishness, the heartlessness, the hypocrisy of the monarchy, the aristocracy, and the church. The old order must fall because it no longer fulfills the ideal for which it was created. It is the judgment of God upon the French people; it is the 'truth clad in hell-fire'; the nation had forgotten God. There are forces in the universe, terrible as the thunder of Sinai, and all nations in all ages are under the same dispensation. No philosophism or encyclopedism, shining in the glittering salons of Paris, could take the place of fundamental religion."[2]

Yes, there is a man with a message that still thunders through the world a century after it was given. What gave him his driving power? Was he born that way?

Carlyle's fiery, crusading spirit and his certainty concerning the judgments of a living God in a moral universe were come the hard way. He passed through a "dark night of the soul." In his autobiographical *Sartor Resartus,* his "Everlasting No" is his synonym for skepticism as to all the values of life. At this period he had little faith and little hope. "My lodestars were blotted out; in that canopy of grim fire shone no star," he wrote. He had "a hot fever of anarchy and misery raving within." "Is there no God, then," he cried, "but at best an absentee God, sitting idle, ever since the first Sabbath, at the outside of his Universe, and *seeing* it go?" In that hour of spiritual despair, "The universe was . . . one huge, dead, immeasurable steam-engine, rolling on, in its dead indifference, to grind me limb from limb."

Then comes his description of an amazing deliverance. ". . . And I

2 *Ibid.,* p. 93.

asked myself 'What *art* thou afraid of? Wherefore, like a coward, dost thou forever pip and whimper, and go cowering and trembling. Despicable biped! What is the sum-total of the worst that lies before thee? Death? Well, Death: and say the pangs of Tophet too and all that the Devil and Man may, will or can do against thee! Hast thou not a heart; canst thou not suffer whatso it be: and, as a Child of Freedom, though outcast, trample Tophet itself under thy feet, while it consumes thee? *Let it come, then; I will meet it and defy it!'* And as I so thought, there rushed like a stream of fire over my whole soul; and I shook base Fear away from me forever. I was strong, of unknown strength; a spirit, almost a god. Ever from that time, the temper of my misery was changed: not Fear or whining Sorrow was it, but Indignation and grim fire-eyed Defiance."

But Carlyle's new-birth was far more than defiance. His chapter on "The Everlasting Yea" is, in my judgment, one of the most stirring in literature. His positive and creative voice now begins to ring. "The universe is not dead and demoniacal, a charnel house with spectres; but godlike, and my Father's! . . . What is nature? . . . Art thou not the Living Garment of God. . . . Love not Pleasure; love God. This is the *Everlasting Yea,* wherein all contradiction is solved."

Comes then the fitting and challenging conclusion to his remarkable transformation. He must help God rebuild the world! "But it is with man's Soul as it was with Nature: the beginning of Creation—Light. . . . The mad primeval Discord is hushed; . . . deep silent rock-foundations are built beneath; and the skyey vault with its ever-lasting Luminaries above; instead of a dark wasteful Chaos, we have a blooming, fertile, heaven-encompassed World. . . . I too could now say to myself: Be not longer a Chaos, but a World. . . . Produce! Produce! Were it but the pitifulest infinitesimal fraction of a Product, produce it in God's name! 'Tis the utmost thou hast in thee; out with it, then. Up, up! Whatsoever thy hand findest to do, do it with thy whole might."

Note carefully what Carlyle did in bringing about his own transformation. He talked to himself like a Dutch uncle! "What art thou afraid of? Wherefore like a coward. . . . Despicable biped!" And squaring off like a fighter at bay he swung into a series of ringing affirmatives which brought him out into his Everlasting Yea—and peace. He was using his critical, judgment-forming conscious mind to read the riot act to his uncritical, cringing, fear-filled unconscious or deep mind which in turn had to accept the new affirmations and bring them into manifestation in the realm of mind, body and affairs. Thus his chaos became a World, and Carlyle a producer of the highest order.

A young man recently came to my study shadowed in gloom and with the everlasting "nay" written all over him. Having been reared in a very conservative church some of his courses in this university had cut his childhood faith from under him and he had lost his courage. His infallible Bible, six-day creation with its Garden of Eden, his literal flaming hell and some other things were slipping from him. He was floundering about in a sea of doubt and despair so that he had lost his zest for study or even for continuing his education.

I put into his hands a copy of my recent book, *Something to Stand On,* a kind of autobiographical story of my own spiritual pilgrimage over the same rough ground but coming out at the end with a positive and everlasting "yea," a place high and lifted up on Christ's own ground where one may plant his feet and stand.

A month later I met this young man on the street. He was a transformed individual if I ever saw one. There was light in his eyes as he drew me out of the traffic and into a quiet doorway. *"Something to Stand On* resolved my doubts and put me back on the track again," he said. "That book did more for me than any other book I ever read. Now I can study again with a purpose." I am casting modesty to the winds in repeating this incident because I suffered the pangs of the very damned for many years as I struggled through to a firm foundation for my own Christian faith, and anything I can say that will induce any troubled student to read that book shall be said in the hope that it will help to bring him through. Because, you see, with a ringing faith in a moral universe and a good God, you can accomplish wonders in spite of anything the world can do to you.

What are *your* habitual assumptions, my friend? Beneath "the maddening maze of things" is there a solid foundation? Is the universe fundamentally friendly? Are there gleams of light in the darkness? Doubts there may be; nor should they be lightly brushed aside by any honest soul. But if there is enough daring within our grasping souls to assume that a good God is at work beneath all the welter and chaos of our struggling world, we too shall eventually crash through to a solid foundation. Let us read over once again Carlyle's "Everlasting Yea" and let its meaning sink deep, deep down into our souls. Then before God, let us resolve to be up and at it! God has no other way to rebuild his shattered world.

LIFE'S BATTLEFIELD

A part of my real compensation, during the fourteen years that we lived in Duluth, lay in our accessibility to the fishing and canoeing country of northern Minnesota. While our boys were still very young it was my happy good fortune to be able to take them with me into that marvelous wilderness where one could travel for days in a noiseless canoe without ever seeing a human being. It was good for the soul of a busy minister and I used to come away from the fragrant pine woods, the sun-dappled portages and the picturesque camp-sites renewed in body, mind and spirit.

On one such trip, however, it turned out to be another story. We had driven north to East Bearskin Lake with a full load of camping equipment and food. As we loaded our big canoe, a few storm clouds appeared, but we thought nothing of it; we had been wet before. Pushing on up the lake we attempted several landings but were horrified to find the ground and trees literally alive with millions of army worms. They had infested the entire country and were stripping the trees of every leaf they possessed.

After much searching we found a small island comparatively free of worms. Being as hungry as bears we tied the canoe to a log that projected into the water and carried our cooking utensils and some food ashore. No sooner had we built our fire, however, than the storm broke in full fury. It picked up blazing pieces of firewood and hurled them into the brush. Jim, Jon and Tom, ages nine, seven and five, flew into action. They whipped off their shirts and raced down to the water and soaked them before I had time to give any directions at all. Then up the bank and onto those fires with wet shirts swinging in every direction. They were like whirling dervishes as the wind bent the trees and whipped up the lake into frothy foam. The waves swept over the canoe, soaking all our equipment and food. Never shall I forget the sight of prunes, bread and cookies floating around on top of the water. I was weary and discouraged—but not my boys. Jim expressed their sentiments exactly when he said: "Gee, Dad, I wouldn't have missed this for the world. This has been the greatest day of my life."

That remark is a commentary on the human race. In the face of trouble and disaster and broken plans, man at his best always rises to meet the difficulty and finds joy in his fight to overcome it. The real satisfaction of life is never found in luxuriously coddled lives, but in men and women who dare and achieve in the face of bitter antagonisms. The greatest personalities of history have tempered their souls in fire. Property loss, sickness and bereavement have been the lot of men from the beginning of time, and the biographies that interest us most are those in which men and women have met the greatest number of seemingly insuperable difficulties and have come through triumphantly. I cannot recall a single outstanding personality who has not been forced to win through to greatness in the face of frowning adversity. The unhappiest world conceivable would be one with nothing hard to do, no conflicts to wage for ends worthwhile; a world where courage and sacrifice were not needed.

I used to have an old gentleman in my congregation who was fond of saying that if he were given the job of creating a world, he would leave out most of the trouble. To all such people we would like to ask several questions. Assuming, as we must, that none of our world rebuilders would want a society of men devoid of strong character, would they leave out the possibility of progress? Or a system of law that is the same for all men? Would they remove free will from mankind? And would they rule out interrelatedness among men?

Of course they would not! And yet most of our troubles in this world stem from those four things. Keep them all in mind while we have a look at "Boss Kettering," vice-president of General Motors and director of their research laboratories. At the age of sixty-nine, after fifty years of invention and research that has changed the face of the whole industrial world, he feels that he is just getting started. Trouble and plenty of it is his idea of the price of all progress. Working his way through Ohio State University as a trouble-shooting mechanic, he nearly went blind by a too strenuous use of his eyes. So he was forced to learn the law of a balanced life—of physical exercise and fresh air to counterbalance his desk work. Working outdoors as a telephone post-hole digger did the business.

Trouble has always dogged his footsteps and prodded him on. While in school he worked out a central battery telephone exchange at Ashland, Ohio, which did away with the nuisance of cranking the phone in rural communities. It should have been a great success but the company decided to scrap the whole thing because the line went dead for about two hours every afternoon. Kettering rushed to the scene and worked feverishly but fruitlessly for days to locate the trouble. He finally found that a certain grandpa had the habit of laying his spectacles on top of the telephone box every afternoon while he took a nap thus short-circuiting the system. "The company people," said Kettering, "were going to throw out their greatest improvement just because they were naturally negative to anything outside their own experience." But do we not all tend to be just that?

Do you remember the spark knock in our auto engines years ago that raised such havoc? Kettering spent fourteen long years on that problem making thousands of experiments. Many of the ingredients that he added to gasoline stopped the knock and stepped up the power but they were too expensive or they chewed up the engine. Fourteen years of trouble; failure after failure; then tetra-ethyl lead and success! "All in research is 99.9 per cent failure and if you succeed once, you're in," he says.

Coming back to our four sources of trouble then, we see that Boss Kettering was kept restless and dissatisfied by his insatiable desire to progress—to accomplish something never attained before; he was bedevilled because the laws of chemistry and physics were immutable and would not bend ever so slightly to fit his momentary needs; he was sore beset because his insatiable thirst for finding a better way caused him freely to choose to keep at the job when others were ready to quit; and finally he never could rest this side of success because so many millions were always in need of his solution to the problem—interdependent men. All of our trouble then stems from these four basic factors in the universe, without any one of which great character would be unattainable.

The one thought that would be totally unsupportable in this life of ours would be that life's pain and hardship and trouble is meaningless and that it has no worthy origin and serves no worthy purpose. Finding it so, we should also find it impossible to believe in a good God. The perennial fascination of Robinson Crusoe lies in the depth of man's soul where it is imperative daily to make the most out of the least. Ole Bull was just another good violin player until his A string snapped as he stood before a packed house in Munich and finished the concert on three strings. Beethoven was just a great composer until, becoming deaf as a post, he kept right on composing superb sonatas. Getting music out of life's remainders after the break has come; writing the sublimest poetry after going blind, as Milton did—that is the human problem in epitome:

> You cannot choose your battlefield,
> The Gods do that for you;
> But you can plant a standard
> Where a standard never flew!

When a soul is winning through to that kind of a solid foundation for life's superstructure, there will be dark days in profusion. Jeremiah was called of God to be a prophet: "I ordained thee a prophet unto the nations," said God to Jeremiah. "Be not afraid of their faces: for I am with thee to deliver thee." Yet this man of God was to see such persecution and trouble that he would cry: "Cursed be the day wherein I was born: let not the day wherein my mother bore me be blessed. . . . Wherefore came I forth out of the womb to see labour and sorrow, that my days should be consumed with shame?" (Jer. 20:14,18) Yet Jeremiah somehow kept his faith in God and became one of the great of earth. Would he have been remembered for three thousand years without his troubles?

In these modern days of exile when millions of displaced persons are wandering the face of the earth, we have a more adequate conception of the sufferings endured in that other exile of the Hebrew people six centuries B.C. Yet listen to this voice from that exile of long ago: "And the ransomed of Jehovah shall return, and come with singing unto Zion; and everlasting joy shall be upon their heads: they shall obtain gladness and joy; and sorrow and sighing shall flee away.

"I, even I, am he that comforteth you: who art thou, that thou art afraid of man that shall die, and the son of man that shall be made as grass; and hast forgotten Jehovah thy maker, that stretched forth the heavens, and laid the foundations of the earth; and fearest continually all the day because of the fury of the oppressor, when he maketh ready to destroy. . . . I have put my words in thy mouth, and have covered thee in the shadow of my hand, that I may plant the heavens, and lay the foundations of the earth, and say unto Zion, Thou art my people." (Isaiah 51:11–16)

It is evident what Isaiah did. He looked straight through the suffering and trouble of the exile and fixed his mind on God and the greatness of God. He reconditioned his fearful and harassed soul by taking it off trouble and resting it in the Eternal. So Grenfell suggested to the man who must live in bleak Labrador, that he would do well to think positively of this land until he discovered its real worth; then he could enjoy battling with the elements. So also, Immanuel Kant, working on a philosophy of life that was to be a turning point in human thought and referring to his incurable illness said: "I have become master of its influence in my thoughts and actions by turning my attention away from this feeling altogether, just as if it did not at all concern me."

Lord Halifax, speaking in the House of Lords some years ago, told about an English country church which carries an inscription to its builder from the time, three hundred years ago, when England was torn by civil war. This inscription reads: "In the year 1643, when all things sacred were either demolished or profaned, this church was built by one whose singular praise it is to have done the best things in the worst times, and to have helped them in the most calamitous."

You thrill, as do I, to the quality of life about which that inscription speaks but let us not let the matter rest there. In this post-war chaos and uncertainty, with mass destitution, suffering and despair all over the world, are we not living in the worst of times? And is God not calling us in tones commanding and impelling to get on the job and to start doing the best things in these worst of times? Do we wring our hands and call to our fellows asking what to do about the secret of the atomic bomb? What to do with the Russians whose way of life is so different and whose attitudes toward its powerful allies always seems so recalcitrant?

What a challenge! What a *glorious* challenge for a Christian nation to start really trusting God for wisdom and guidance so that some future historian may say of us what Thucydides said of certain men of his day who "dared beyond their strength, hazarded against their judgment, and in extremities were of excellent hope."

So it was with Staff Sergeant Jacob D. Deshazer, one of the Doolittle fliers. Shot down and imprisoned by the Japanese, he suffered from malnutrition and abuse for forty-one long months. During that time he wrote his mother that "the Japs haven't had a chance spiritually" and he proposed to train to become a Christian missionary and to go back to Japan with the message of Christ.

The best things in the worst times . . . ! What a day this is to be a dispenser of the unsearchable riches of Christ!

LIFE'S DIVIDENDS

Some time ago in Billy Rose's column was food for thought. He related that in 1923 a group of the world's most successful financiers met at the Edgewater Beach Hotel in Chicago. Collectively these tycoons controlled more wealth than there was in the U.S. Treasury, and for years newspaper and magazines had been printing their success stories as good examples for the youth of America to follow. They were the Horatio Alger success boys.

Twenty-five years later this was the score: The president of the largest independent steel company—Charles M. Schwab—lived on borrowed money the last five years of his life, and died broke; the greatest wheat speculator—Arthur Cutten—died insolvent; the president of the N.Y. Stock Exchange—Richard Whitney—had just been released from prison; Albert Fall, a member of the President's cabinet, had just been released from prison so he could die at home; the greatest "man" in Wall Street—Jesse Livermore—had committed suicide; Leon Fraser, president of the Bank of International Settlement, had also committed suicide.

In closing his review of this sad record Billy Rose remarked that all of these men had learned how to make money but they had not learned how to live. At the time of their famous dinner in the Edgewater Beach Hotel they were considered the world's greatest experts in *stock* dividends but twenty-five years later they had demonstrated that they knew very little about *life's* dividends.

One of the most important questions that any young person can ask himself is: What do I really want from life? And the answer would seem to be fairly simple: I want the deepest satisfaction available. Stock dividends are important but life dividends are more so. The only lasting satisfactions come from loving and helping people, from doing one's share in fighting inequality and injustice in the building of the good society which Jesus called the Kingdom of God.

Freedom of the press is one of the prize inheritances from the past. Yet in our legitimate zeal to cope with the enemy of Communism we are in danger of losing this and all other freedoms. When the *Nation* was recently banned from the New York public schools for printing Paul Blanshard's series of articles on the Catholic Church, a group of brave citizens formed the Stop Censorship Committee and presented the Board of Superintendents the following thrilling statement by Burgess Meredith:

On November 24, 1644, the poet, John Milton, addressed these words to the Parliament of England: ". . . as good almost to kill a man as kill a good book—who kills a man kills a reasonable creature, God's image, but he who destroys a good book kills reason itself . . . kills the image of God—as it were—in the eye."

We declare ourselves guardians of the wisdom of the blind poet, Milton. Art, science, and philosophy—"the breath of the reason itself"—is our heritage. We announce our faith in liberty and our own determination to fight for respect for the individual and his freedom to develop and express his creativity to the full.

Throughout the ages, pigmy men have tried in vain by use of the cup of hemlock, the arena of wild animals, the stake, the rack and screw, the branding iron, the guillotine, the dungeon, the firing squad, and the crematorium to close men's mouths, stay their hands, shut tight their minds. The pigmies are the nameless of the shadows of history. Modern inquisitors, do you know the name Socrates? They censored him! Have you heard of Michaelangelo, of Galileo, da Vinci, Dante, Beethoven, Molière, Balzac, Zola, Goya, Rousseau, Paine, Cervantes, Ibsen, Whitman, Thoreau, Emerson, Darwin? These men were censored!

Can you name their inquisitors? Can you name the un-something committee on which they served?

In considering life's dividends each of us would do well to ponder whether we prefer to stand with the forgotten inquisitors—or with the illustrious company they sought to silence. A fresh opportunity to join one company or the other is ours nearly every day.

We are frequently called upon to stand up and be counted in the battle for racial justice. A recent episode in this struggle took place in St. Louis with the local bar association. Sidney R. Redmond, a Harvard graduate and an outstanding Negro lawyer, was recommended for membership by the association's committee on admissions. Jacob M. Lashly, a former president of the American Bar Association, led the debate in favor of admitting Mr. Redmond, stating:

"It is my distinct and profound feeling that Redmond is entitled to fair rating and consideration on his merits. I am not a white man through any merit of my own. I was born that way. Redmond is a man of culture and high character and he has brought to the bar no dishonor. He is a credit to his race and our profession."

Redmond's application failed of approval by fifteen votes: an applicant must receive approval by more than four-fifths of the total vote. One outstanding member, Max W. Kramer, resigned because of this action, declaring:

"He (Redmond) was good enough for the Harvard law school and good enough to be elected an alderman. He enjoys an excellent reputation as a lawyer and is a representative and respected citizen in the community. There can be only one reason for his being denied membership in the bar association and that is the color of his skin. That reason is not good enough for me."

I fancy Mr. Kramer went home to dinner that night with one of life's choicest dividends securely locked in his heart.

Most of us start out early in life in possession of some very high ideals and with a determination to do our part in the realization of our high standards. Then what Channing Pollock once called "the world's slow stain" creeps in and by middle age we have become disillusioned by retreat after retreat and by repeated compromise. Wordsworth stated the case for us all:

> Heaven lies about us in our infancy!
> Shades of the prison-house begin to close
> Upon the growing boy,
> But he beholds the light, and whence it flows,

He sees it in his joy.
The youth, who daily farther from the east
Must travel, still is Nature's priest,
And by the vision splendid
Is on his way attended.
At length the man perceives it die away,
And fade into the light of common day.

Some people allow ill health to rob them of the joys of accomplishment. With vitality at low ebb they step out of the stream of life and join the ranks of the complainers. Others remain on the top level of thought, feeling and acting in spite of their trouble. Robert Louis Stevenson was such a man. Listen to the part of a letter he wrote from his lonely island in the South Pacific in 1893:

For fourteen years I have not had one day of real health. I have awakened sick and gone to bed weary, and yet I have done my work unflinchingly. I have written my books in bed and out of bed, written them when I was torn by coughing, written them during hemorrhages, written them when my head swam from weakness. I have now done this for so long that it seems to me I have won the wager and recovered my glove! But the battle still goes on—ill or well is a trifle so long as it goes.

It was from his bed that he wrote one of his most thoughtful essays on "The Technical Elements of Style." When eye trouble forced him to stay in a darkened room he still wrote on in the diminished light. He scrawled some of his gayest poems in *A Child's Garden of Verses* after a severe hemorrhage forced him to put his right arm in a sling. After all, he still had his left arm! Even when he became so ill the doctor forbade him to write or talk he actually tried to dictate, in the deaf and dumb alphabet, the remainder of the book he was writing!

Now how in the world does a man get that way? With the fates so pitilessly concentrated against him how did Stevenson manage to go on extracting so many choice dividends out of life? The answer would seem to be that he deliberately turned the stream of his consciousness away from self and out into the world of men. In his books and poetry he was out there with them fighting the battle for his ideals and always winning. He identified himself with every good thought and movement in the world to such an extent that his darkened sick room ceased to exist for long periods of time. The result was a demonstration of Jesus' deep word of wisdom: "he that loses his life for my sake and the gospel's shall find it."

Out in Bristol, Connecticut, Maurice C. and William H. Smith who own the Bristol Manufacturing Corporation have learned the secret. Two years ago William Smith went to his brother and said: "All we think about is making a profit. Let's do something totally unselfish. Let's have one department in the business that is concerned solely with doing good." The result a few days later was the appointment of Dr. Dale D. Dutton of the Central Baptist Church in Providence as "Vice President in Charge of Doing Good." The only orders he has are: "Go out and do good and take orders from nobody but God."

Backed by a sizeable budget, Dr. Dutton has shuttled back and forth across the nation for two years helping people in trouble. One week he may be in Dallas pleading for support of the Community Chest; the next in Chicago to talk with a man on the point of deserting his wife and children. Thousands of letters are referred to Dr. Dutton every week. One came from a man on trial for his life in Portsmouth, Virginia, and Dr. Dutton found evidence which proved that the man had been framed. Another in the same mail from a Vermont farm lad read: "I've got a scholarship to a good private school but my only clothes are a pair of worn overalls." That boy entered school with an adequate wardrobe. The Smiths admit that Dr. Dutton has the most interesting and challenging job in the firm and the one they would prefer to have.

Every one of us can establish a department of doing good in our own lives in a thousand different ways. Sophie Shanks is a cheerful, God-fearing Negro woman whose only contact with luxury is her night job as floor-polisher in Cincinnati's Netherland-Plaza Hotel. She gets home from work in the morning in time to send the eldest of nine children off to school, and to greet her husband as he leaves their tenement flat for his garbage truck job.

Not long ago she received a letter that read: "When I was in Cincinnati this spring, my helpers informed me that you are a deserving lady who works hard on the night shift . . . and that you have a tough time raising your nine children . . . but you never complain. . . . So here's a check for one hundred dollars." It was signed "Santa Claus" and the Los Angeles bank on which it was drawn honored it.

The bank president says the anonymous Santa Claus is constantly sending checks to the Sophie Shanks of the nation and deriving great satisfaction therefrom.

Financial dividends are a reward usually paid a person some time after an original investment has had time to accumulate them. Life's dividends of satisfaction likewise must be preceded by a definite investment of one's self in some area of human need. No investment, no returns. Large investment, large returns. Had any dividends lately?

MADE IN THIS IMAGE

Not long ago, a graduate student and his attractive young wife came to my study for a talk about God. "I am soon to take a Ph.D. here at S.U.I.," he said, "but the joy and zest for work has been progressively evading me as I have been losing my belief in God. My basic purpose for living has disappeared in the process."

That young man is in the same boat with thousands of other university students. They have lost their childhood God of the Big Man in the sky who supposedly upset the processes of cosmic law to work miracles for His "good" children but they have not found a Creator who can be considered intellectually respectable by an educated individual.

Nevertheless, the footprints of God in this wonderful universe are as clear as daylight when properly interpreted. The day that Robinson Crusoe gazed at a footprint in the sands on the island of Juan Fernandez, he rightly considered that a man must have planted his foot there. As he looked around he could not see this man but he was not surprised later on to confront "Friday" in the flesh.

The great astronomer, Kirchner, had a friend who was having his doubts about the existence of God. When that friend called one day and noticed a globe of the world which Kirchner had made and placed in his study, he asked the astronomer who made it. "Why," said Kirchner, "it made itself." As the friend laughed heartily at this joke, the astronomer said: "You laugh at that as absurd, and rightly so. But it would be a thousand times easier to believe that this little globe made itself than that the large one on which we live made itself."

Let your mind travel out and out in a vast sweep of our illimitable starry universe. The nearest star, Proxima Centauri, is 25 billion miles away. Light from that star, traveling 186,000 miles per second, reaches the earth in 33 hours. Light from Betelgeuse, whose diameter is 273,000,000 miles, reaches the earth in about 100 years. Then reflect that our largest telescope catches light from stars so far away that it has been traveling one billion years at that terrific speed! Yet all of these millions of stars are obeying star law so exactly that astronomers can tell where any given star will be at 4 P.M. one hundred years from today.

Now bring the mind back and consider the atom which is a small solar system in itself. Around its central nucleus of positive electricity, called a proton, the electrons revolve as the planets revolve around the sun. Electrons move in an orbit of less than one millionth of an inch in diameter, but they make the circuit several thousand million times a second!

These atoms are as porous as the solar system. If we eliminated all the unfilled space in a man's body, and collected his protons and electrons into one mass, that man would be reduced to a speck just visible with a magnifying glass. So says Arthur S. Eddington, world-renowned physicist, in his epochal book, *The Nature of the Physical Universe*.

Atoms, which are the building blocks of the starry universe as well as of the material world in which we live and have our being, obey cosmic law and thereby constitute the foundation of a *dependable universe*. Were this not true we should have chaos instead of a universe.

When we have said, however, that everything in the universe must obey cosmic law we have not explained the ultimate cause of any phenomenon. We have merely said: Given certain conditions you will always get certain results because of cosmic law. It is not the province of science to ask *why*. All the scientist is supposed to do is to ask: *What are the facts?* It is the province of philosophy and religion to ask why. And when we ask why, we conclude that a law implies *a law-giver or maker*.

When we drive our cars down a city street and come to a sign

that reads "stop," we rightly conclude that that sign was put there
for all men to obey. It is the law, and back of that law are *lawmakers*
with the purpose of saving lives and property. If we obey the law
everything works beautifully. If we violate the law we are in trouble
and must pay the penalty.

At this point I can hear someone say: "All very interesting but I
still do not see very much purpose back of the laws governing the
atom." So let us look again.

Here is a blade of grass. A chemist can break it up into its con-
stituent parts and find carbon, nitrogen, hydrogen, oxygen, iron,
chlorine, phosphorus, sodium, potassium and silicon. But the greatest
chemist in the world cannot take those chemicals and make a blade
of grass. But Someone can do it by using the sun and a process called
photosynthesis. The Greek word "photos" means light and "synthesis"
means to put together. A mysterious something they call chlorophyll
uses the sun's rays to transmute all of these lifeless chemical elements into *living matter*. How do the molecules of chlorophyll perform this miracle? Nobody knows. It is a secret that the greatest
scientists in the world are unable to penetrate. All they know is that
Something or Someone does know how to transmute lifeless matter
into living matter.

But come further. When this process has produced a dandelion and
this beautiful little flower has lived out its little day and the life
principle is safely hid in the seed, certain molecules arrange themselves in such a way as to make an ingenious little parachute. New
ground must be found so the new plant can repeat the miracle of
photosynthesis the next spring. At a given moment when the wind is
just right, Someone calls, "Cast off," and the little seed soars aloft
and is easily carried to its new home. Why some molecules arrange
themselves in the seed and others make themselves into a parachute
is a mystery, but the whole process is an "intelligent" one.

Have a good look at a feather. In a single pinion of an eagle's
wing there are nearly a million different parts. There are the barbules
which give the feather its essential character both as an organ of
flight and as a covering to preserve the heat of the body. Each
barbule is made up of thousands of cells, varying considerably in
order to give strength and elasticity to the whole web. No two
feathers in an eagle's wing are alike, yet, taken together, they make

up one of the most effective flight machines that can be imagined.

One is forced to ask oneself what *directive* power guides the distribution of the molecules that go into the making of the many kinds of feathers on an eagle's body; what directing intelligence makes blood out of the food an eagle eats and then uses that blood to make, not only feathers, but bones, muscles, beaks, eyes and claws. Or why it is that a thousand different birds can eat the same food and yet be so different?

Scientists tell us that ultramicroscopic genes and their companions, the chromosomes, inhabit every living cell and are the absolute keys to all human, animal and vegetable characteristics. We are stunned when they tell us that a thimbleful would hold all the genes of all the more than two billion people that live on this earth. Yet these same genes contain the determinants of all of the two billions of human beings on earth! How a few million atoms, locked up in an ultramicroscopic gene can rule all life on earth is an example of profound intelligence and cunning that could emanate only from an infinitely Creative Intelligence.

It is at this point that the atheist finds himself on untenable ground. If there is no purpose or guiding Intelligence back of the phenomena we have been discussing what is the answer? The atheist says it all "happens"; it is a "fortuitous concourse of atoms going it blind." That does not make sense.

One summer my boys and I were crossing a portage between lakes in the wilds of Canada. In the path about halfway across lay a rifle. Its rusted condition brought us to the conclusion that someone had lost it out of his pack toward the close of the previous season; that before the man lost it, the steel and wood of the rifle had been cleverly put together in a factory by other men who had the purpose of manufacturing a shooting iron. Was that not a more sensible conclusion than to say that it all just happened. That the steel and wood somehow got together in that portage by accident?

The footprints of God or Creative Intelligence seem to most of us to be fairly plain everywhere in the universe. When we come to man, however, we come upon phenomena that are found nowhere else. We say he is a living soul. He can think and feel and will and he has an innate sense of oughtness that we call a conscience. Man alone can think and make reasoned judgments. A scientist may gaze forever at

the visible brain of a man and speculate endlessly about the special-
ized molecules and atoms that compose that brain, but he cannot
tell us how a man uses those atoms in the process of thought. Nor
can he explain why some men will deliberately decide to give up
their lives rather than lie or murder or steal; nor why still others will
gladly sacrifice their lives in order to save some other life.

Come back with me, for example, to Christmas morning in the
year 1809. There in Danville, Kentucky, on the edge of the wilderness is a young physician by the name of Ephraim McDowell. He is
stoking the fire to be sure there is plenty of hot water, for he is
preparing to perform the first abdominal operation in history. Sitting
there in the chair is Mrs. Thomas Crawford suffering from a huge
tumor in her abdomen. She has made an agonizing journey of sixty
miles on horseback in the hope that her life may be saved.

Yes, she knows that most people consider cutting into the
abdominal cavity would be just plain murder. That is what the mob
thinks outside the house. For word has somehow spread that young
Dr. McDowell is going to try to cut this tumor out and the mob has
let it be known that if the patient dies they will hang the doctor.
They have the rope over the limb of a tree in the yard and they are
ready. After all, men had been hung for less than that in Daniel
Boone's Kentucky.

But Dr. McDowell went straight ahead with his operation and
the patient lived, and an important milestone was passed in the
history of medicine. So we ask why. Why was McDowell determined
to risk his own life to save another? The answer is because of an insistent inner voice that kept whispering, if we may paraphrase the
words of du Noüy in *Human Destiny: You shall be ready to suffer
and to give your life rather than abandon your ideals. No longer are
your principle aims to live and eat. For noble ends you will endure
hunger and death. And you must be noble for that is the will of the
new being who has arisen in you.*

You cannot derive living from non-living matter, nor the intelligent
from the non-intelligent, nor the moral from the non-moral. So our
minds insist on asking whence came life, intelligence and morality?
To most of us the atheist exhibits an amazing credulity by assuming
that these things just happened; that they came from nowhere and
are going nowhere. We find it more logical to believe that they are to

be found in the Being of a Creator; that living, intelligent, moral men derive these qualities from Someone they call God.

And now hang on tight as we round the bend and sail straight into the most amazing, inspiring, challenging idea that it is possible for our minds to conceive: You and I were *made in the mold and image of the Creative Intelligence and Eternal Love that we call God! We too possess unbelievable creative power. Every thought creates!*

Listen to this: "In the beginning was the Word, and the Word was with God, and *the Word was God.* All things were made by him; and without him was not any thing made that was made. In him was life; and the life was the light of men" (John 1:1–4). A word is a symbol of thought. John is telling us that all creation is the result of the *thoughts* of Infinite Mind and Creative Intelligence.

Now come on to this: *"And God said, Let us make man in our image, after our likeness and let them have dominion . . . over all the earth. . . . So God created man in his own image . . ."* (Genesis 1:26–27). Let us carry that thought with us. We are the possessors of unbelievable Creative Power through the thoughts that we hold in our minds. *We are Individuated Centers of the One Creative Life and Power!* Use that affirmation repeatedly to drive the idea into the deep mind.

THE CREATIVE IMAGE

Countless numbers of people whose names are on some church roll no longer pray. It is not that they do not want to pray but rather that they have long since ceased to believe that it did any good. They have perhaps read of some devout mother who prayed for the safety of her son on the battlefield only to learn of his death. They have known of people begging God for this or that as though He were a Cosmic Errand Boy ready to run here and there in the universe to do their bidding and they have lost faith, and rightly so, in that kind of God.

Such people need to know their Bibles better and come to understand the progressive unfolding there portrayed of the relationship between God and man. The Old Testament begins with men fearing an awful Monarch who must needs be placated and bought through bargaining, wheedling, and through the presentation of sacrifices and gifts. As He sat on His throne far away in the sky, He could be influenced by the gifts of bullocks, sheep and goats. The blood of these sacrifices was supposed to be especially efficacious in calming God's anger.

But there was a progressive revelation of God to his children as fast as they were able to receive it which is reflected in the great prophetic period of Jeremiah, Isaiah, Ezekiel and Amos and which finally comes to full flower in Jesus. The Heavenly Father of Jesus was not an august monarch far away in the skies but a loving, radiant, energizing Spirit whose kingdom of heaven is within. The power and joy of this inner Kingdom could be realized and appropriated, not by animal sacrifices or gifts, not by begging, but by communion and quiet contemplation, by the repeated use of the creative imaging power of the mind focused on the love, understanding and forgiveness of the Eternal Presence.

Mere words cannot describe the healing, therapeutic values that accrue to any mind that gives itself to creative contemplation and communion. Does a young man deeply in love with a beautiful girl go to a dictionary to find out what a kiss is? If he does he reads that "to kiss is to smack with the pursed lips (a compression of the closed cavity of the mouth by the cheeks giving a slight sound when the rounded contact of the lips with one another is broken)." Would our ardent young lover read those words, roll his eyes heavenward and then tell himself he now knows what a kiss is? Neither can words adequately describe prayer. All the minister can do is to try and describe it in such a way that his hearers will want to enter into the experience themselves.

Again and again, Jesus, weary and worn, withdrew into the woods, the desert, the mountains or the seashore to be alone with God. In these times of blessed communion he was seeking contact with the sources of being, in touch with that greater consciousness which reactivates our hidden springs of health and happiness. There he was not repeating the set prayers and invocations of the synagogue; he was in intimate and vital contact with God through silent communion; through the intense focusing of his imaging power of the love and radiance of the Indwelling Presence.

Prayer at its best is not begging. It is communion, longing, visualization of the constructive release of our higher capacities. It is the process of quietly and deliberately choosing a ruling attitude based on love and confidence in the Creator of a friendly universe which brings spiritual unity and harmony to the center of being.

Modern psychology has shown that the will obeys the imagination because the imaging power is stronger than will power. It is the image in the mind that gives form and content to purpose. Thus if we would change in attitude from negative to positive, an inner change must first come in the imagination.

Paul lists certain fruits of the spirit that are also mental creations: "Finally, brethren, whatsoever things are true, whatsoever things are honest, whatsoever things are just, whatsoever things are pure, whatsoever things are lovely, whatsoever things are of good report . . . *think* on these things." (Phil. 4:8) He says that "the peace of God which passeth all understanding, shall keep our *hearts* and *minds* through Christ Jesus."

How does the peace of God keep one's heart and mind through Christ? By relaxing in some quiet place and visualizing the radiance and love of Christ. Jesus, having lived the God-conscious life upon earth, was the perfect revelation of God. By his own constant use of functional imagery centering in God, Jesus revealed himself as a master of the technique of reaching this inner level of life. His will followed his God-centered imagination. His constant demand that his followers "only believe," only "have faith as a grain of mustard seed," was conditioned on his knowledge of these forces.

When a lunatic boy was brought to Jesus after the disciples had failed to cure him, his father knelt before Jesus and pled for the touch of his healing hand on the lad. When Jesus healed him, the disciples asked why they had failed. "Because of your unbelief," said the Master, "for verily, I say unto you, If ye have faith as a grain of mustard seed, ye shall say unto a mountain, Remove hence to yonder place and it shall remove; and nothing shall be impossible unto you."

Let us not take this literally as many have done or we will miss the point completely. I know of a man who thought he would try it out, so he commanded a high sand dune on the shore of Lake Michigan to remove itself so he could have an unobstructed view of the lake.

When the dune refused to budge he declared he was through with prayer forever! Jesus used hyperbole, a legitimate form of exaggeration, to portray a spiritual truth.

Strong belief in the inevitability of disaster has the power to bring disaster into manifestation by the use of the same law. Nicholas II, Czar of Russia, was conditioned in boyhood to believe that his reign would be involved in an endless series of tragic accidents. He was told that he was born on the day of Job and that nothing he would ever do would be a success. A monk told him his reign would be full of poverty, war and rebellion. The emperor therefore faced every undertaking with fear, suspicion and doubt. I have read his tragic life with great care and I am convinced that a strong man of faith could have avoided most of the tragedy of his reign through courageous and constructive leadership.

At this point someone may say: "You talk as if prayer were merely auto-suggestion." And when someone says that, he usually implies that auto-suggestion cannot be undergirded and supported by objective reality. Auto-suggestion is merely suggestion made by oneself to oneself concerning what he believes to be true. If I say, "I believe in God" or "I believe in the accuracy of the multiplication table," I am engaging in auto-suggestion but no one should conclude that my suggestions to myself thereby lack objective validity. Let us have done with the fearful bugaboo of "auto-suggestion." Of course we use it. We cannot practice faith and belief without it. The thing for us to keep definitely in mind is that *the mental imaging that accompanies either a positive or a negative approach to any statement will bring its own kind into manifestation. It is the law of the mind. It is the way God works.*

Little children put their imaginations into everything they do. Therefore Jesus gave the whole law of alignment when he commanded us to turn and become as little children if we would experience the Kingdom of heaven here and now. The fact that we must make certain suggestions to ourselves in appropriating this Kingdom does not imply that this Kingdom is not eternally true.

Let us not let the fear of the word "auto-suggestion" rob us of the power and presence of God. "Be ye transformed by the renewing of your mind," said Paul. A mind is renewed by holding the mental image of a divine influx of love and radiance straight out of the heart of God. To live thus is to relax and go *with* the current, *with* life as it flows through us, making our lives a living channel of the divine. And the one thing that will check it is skepticism and doubt and disbelief. Even Jesus could do little for people who were negative in their thinking.

Bertrand Russell in his *Philosophical Essays* some years ago concluded that science makes it impossible for an intelligent man to believe in God or in any benign purpose back of the universe:

Such in outline, but even more purposeless, more void of meaning, is the world which Science presents for our belief. Amid such a world, if anywhere, our ideals henceforward must find a home. . . . Blind to good and evil, reckless of destruction, omnipotent matter rolls on its relentless way; for man, condemned today to lose his dearest, tomorrow himself to pass through the gate of darkness, it remains only to cherish, ere yet the blow falls, the lofty thoughts that ennoble his little day; . . . to worship at the shrine his own hands have built; . . . to sustain alone, a weary but unyielding Atlas, the world that his own ideals have fashioned despite the trampling march of unconscious power.

Let a man believe *that* and he automatically robs himself of any possibility of attaining a state of health, happiness or peace. By deliberately choosing this negative and paralyzing view of life, he robs himself of the basic security without which he can never truly live. Fortunately many great men of science have, in recent decades, given the lie to Bertrand Russell's position. They say that the further they travel the scientific road, the more evident it becomes that there is something akin to Mind and Purpose back of everything that is; that the Christian belief in God is not only intellectually respectable but a prime necessity for living the good life.

Take a brief look at the "Little Professor of Piney Woods." Lawrence Clifton Jones, Missouri-born Negro, graduated from the University of Iowa in 1907. Although offered a number of good positions, he turned them all down and headed south into Mississippi because he wanted to do something constructive for his people. In the heart of the piney woods south of Jackson he started teaching with three illiterate Negro boys as his "school."

Friends gave him land and money and he soon had a large number of pupils learning arithmetic by figuring profits on good crops and well-cared-for livestock. They learned good English by writing essays about sound farming. He taught them how to work with their hands and minds, how to visualize success and how to get along with each other. The school grew and grew until today there are five handsome brick structures and sixty frame buildings and thirty teachers. A steady stream of competent graduates going out into life to help still other Negro children to prepare for the better life has made the Little Professor of Piney Woods known from one end of our country to the other. The governor of Mississippi has called him "one of the first citizens of Mississippi."

When someone asked Lawrence Jones how he managed to persevere through the long years of his early struggle he said: "I just kept on praying as if everything depended on God, and kept working as if everything depended on me. You can't get discouraged if you do that."

Think about that statement for a moment. Here was a man practicing the "single eye" philosophy of Jesus: "If thine eye be single thy whole body shall be full of light." Lawrence Jones kept tuned to the God of hope, truth, beauty, goodness and success. He left no time or place for the stream of his consciousness to turn in upon himself or to dwell upon failure. He loved every one of those ignorant and poor Negro children, and he never doubted for a single moment but that he could help them to help themselves.

Take another example. When Ruth Moulton retired from active teaching in the eastern school which she and her husband had run for forty-four years, she was asked to tell of the most thrilling experience she could recall during her long term of service. Without a moment's hesitation she said it concerned the healing experience of Dr. Sara Deford, now an assistant professor of English at an eastern college.

Sara was fourteen at the beginning of the story. One day her mother appeared in Mrs. Moulton's office and, under deep emotion, stated that a recent diagnosis of Sara's eyes had indicated that she was slowly going blind. Sara was not to be told the dreadful truth but the mother thought Mrs. Moulton might make allowances for poor work as time progressed.

Early one lovely autumn morning Mrs. Moulton met Sara on top of a near-by hill where, it transpired, each had gone for quiet meditation and prayer. It was there that Sara told her principal of her secret, of how she had overheard the doctor tell her mother of the steady advance of Sara's blindness and of his inability to arrest the progress of the disease. "But don't tell mother I know," cautioned Sara, "for it would only worry her still more."

As a result of that chance meeting, an early morning prayer group was soon meeting in Mrs. Moulton's office, attended by Sara and some of the other girls. The influence of that group of girls produced a harmonious and peaceful atmosphere that permeated the entire school as they all prayed for the healing of Sara's eyes by holding her lovingly in their Heavenly Father's embrace.

Let us quote Mrs. Moulton's words on the final result: "Months later the eye doctor noticed a sudden change in Sara's eyes. A change for the better. We held our breath. The next examination showed still further improvement. At the end of three years the progressive nearsightedness had completely stopped." No part of the human body can ever be separated from the healing power of faith.

Stand guard then, dear friends, at the threshold of consciousness and keep all negative thinking outside. Dare to visualize Christ, the true, the good, and the beautiful and to affirm that his power is also yours—now. Dream great dreams and make great claims in the name of God and have the courage to act as if they were true *now*. Proof of the vitality and eternal reality of this way of life will come with the splendor of the blazing noonday sun and you will be worshiping the Father in spirit and in truth.

THE PERSONALITY OF JESUS

"Christianity is the most pious fraud in history," said Nietsche. He affirmed that Christian teaching made strength a devil and weakness a god. He saw a troop of Prussian cavalry marching to the front one day and at that moment, he tells us, his philosophy took shape. "I felt for the first time that the strongest and highest Will to Life does not find expression in a miserable struggle for existence but in a Will to War, a Will to Power, a Will to Overpower."

Adolf Hitler, personally as weak and frustrated in his younger days as was Friedrich Wilhelm Nietsche, adopted Nietsche's philosophy.

The Nazis made a new Bible of their own—a Bible that glorified brute strength and the superman above all else. "Christianity is for women and children," said a blond young German boy to me in the summer of 1939 in Hannover. "We men have no time for church; we must utilize our time on Sunday mornings to learn to make war."

Now Hitler and his cohorts are dead, and Europe is a shambles, but the Christ he repudiated stands as unshaken as ever. He has met and challenged and defeated other philosophies of life for more than nineteen centuries, emerging after each conflict more quietly sure than ever.

It is true that many have sought to portray the Nazarene as "Gentle Jesus, meek and mild." Artists have drawn him with a lamb in his arms or with little children playing about him. And this indeed represents one distinguishing mark of his many-sided personality. But weakness? Never under the shining sun! Ernest Renan, the French writer, wrote a "Life of Jesus" in 1863 in which he said: "His lovely character, and doubtless one of those transporting countenances which sometimes appear in the Jewish race, created around him a circle of fascination. Tenderness of heart was in him transformed into infinite sweetness, vague poetry, universal charm."

Jesus, far from being essentially meek and mild, exuding an atmosphere of "vague poetry," *confronted the world with the most radical philosophy of personal and social life that it had ever had*. He watched the Pharisees striving to obey over six hundred rules of conduct whose inner significance they had never known or had long since forgotten, while they evinced no particular concern over justice, humility and mercy. He saw them callously shortchanging the poor in the Temple Court and, with blazing eyes that would brook no interference, he drove them out singlehanded. He called them hypocrites and whited sepulchres, sons of hell. Nothing weak about that!

He talked about the lilies he saw growing in the fields as evidence of a loving Heavenly Father's creative power; about sparrows being unable to fall without that Father observing it; about a God-Presence that would burst through all previous conceptions as new wine bursts old bottles or as a new patch fails to fit an old garment. He demonstrated his friendship for the forgotten and the despised and said it were better for a millstone to be hanged about a man's neck and that he be drowned in the deepest sea rather than that he offend "one of these little ones." He told matchless stories about shepherds leaving their sheep safely tucked away in the sheepfold at night while the shepherd went back into the hills to search for the one that was lost. He told of a woman searching her house diligently until she found a lost coin. All of these wonderful stories were told to point up and sharpen his teaching concerning the worth of every human being in the sight of his Father.

But he also called himself an *incendiary:* "I came to cast fire upon the earth." Fire consumes whatever opposes it and the evil that opposes Jesus' Way of Life would be consumed. He called himself and his truth a stone: "He that falleth on this stone shall be broken in pieces: but on whomsoever it shall fall it will scatter him as dust." Mussolini, Hitler, and their kind now know what he meant! Having said that, however, with all of the conviction and force at his command, he then went on to call himself a physician whose chief concern was curing the spiritually sick. The Father wants no man to be scattered as dust but each one, being free, must choose the way of life that he will follow.

He was not particularly interested in rules of conduct even though some rules may be necessary. He was emphatic about certain *principles* and above all his emphasis was upon the love of God and the love of man which would automatically eventuate in right conduct. "Ye are the *salt* of the earth." "Ye are the *light* of the world." Salt was a basic preservative in a warm country where food spoiled unless it was protected by something that permeated the whole. Light was something that automatically destroyed darkness.

After using "salt" and "light" to describe the God-consciousness which was basic in his Way of Life he went on to illustrate how this principle within operated: "Ye have heard that it was said by them of old time, Thou shalt not kill. . . . But I say unto you that whosoever is angry with his brother without a cause shall be in danger of hell fire." Becoming angry and calling names was the thing that led to strife and murder. Jesus got back to root causes. "Ye have heard that it was said by them of old time, Thou shalt not commit adultery: But I say unto you that whosoever looketh on a woman to lust after her hath committed adultery with her already in his heart." He went back of the rule to the root cause of the violation and showed the important thing to be clean, controlled thinking. This does not mean that we are not to think, honestly and unafraid, about sex. The old hush, hush prohibition on this subject has done incalculable harm. You might as well tell a man never to think about food. But it does demand controlled, intelligent thinking.

He faced in his contemporaries an ethic of rules and regulations that fussed endlessly over the small and unimportant things while neglecting that which was basic and important. Against this externalism of rules and regulations, he pleaded for a life inwardly right because it does not hate and does not commit adultery because it does not revel in obscene imagery. He pleaded for a positive life of active enthusiasm for great causes of human betterment, enthusiastic because it was permeated by the radiant, selfless, dynamic power which he described as the Kingdom of God which was within.

Jesus was no "meek and mild" individual. He was gentle and loving and full of deep understanding and strength. His Way of Life was expressly meant for this tough, sinful, cruel world where ill-will and injustice inspire a return of still greater ill-will and injustice that can but end in chaos and death. Jesus' Way is a rugged Way that calls for character, strength and courage that come only from faith in God.

How graphically he illustrated all of this when he "set his face" to go to Jerusalem where he knew full well his pious, rule-dominated enemies would kill him. He was walking south toward Jerusalem and came to the outskirts of Samaria. The Samaritans hated the Jews of Jerusalem and so they refused to let him pass through their city. James and John flew into a rage and asked permission to call down fire from heaven to consume them. But Jesus "rebuked them" and said, "Ye know not what manner of spirit ye are of," as he took another route. These disciples, though they had been with him for three years, still had much to learn about Christ's Way of Life.

He likewise demonstrated his principles in the way he handled Zacchaeus the tax-gatherer. He did not say: "You grafting, selfish, hypocritical little Jew—come down out of that tree and let me tell you something." No, he smiled and invited himself to Zacchaeus' house to lunch. The radiance and the understanding that emanated from Jesus' presence called silently to the little grafter to repent and change his whole attitude toward life. Zacchaeus found salvation that lovely day.

What magic results come from following through with the principles Jesus emphasized. Henry M. Stanley's early life was full of bitterness. The man who was later to find David Livingstone in Africa never knew his father. He was disowned by his mother, and the Asaph workhouse where he labored was a place of misery and cruelty. When he heard some pious hypocrite lead devotions there and read, "Little children . . . love one another," he wondered what it meant. Though his child heart yearned for love, he began to think that the most beautiful passages in the Bible were wholly inapplicable to life. He had come, even as a child, to disbelieve in love.

Then one day the fugitive boy who had run away from his ship in New Orleans stood in front of a kind, grave gentleman who had taken him into his store and then into his home. The man took a basin of water, made the sign of the cross on his brow, gave him his own name, Henry M. Stanley, and then gathered the lad into his big strong arms and kissed him. His senses whirled and reeled under the impact of this genuine expression of a strong man's love, and tears, which no amount of cruelty had ever forced from him, poured down his cheeks. "The golden period of my life began from that supreme moment," he said.

The stature of Abraham Lincoln increases with every year in the direct ratio that we come to appreciate his personification of qualities of Christlikeness. On one occasion he called at McClellan's home to consult him about a military matter. The general had gone to a reception. After a considerable wait, the general returned and went up to bed even though he had been told that Lincoln was waiting for an interview.

The President of the United States finally went home with a heavy heart but he never spoke of this incident to McClellan's enemies. When the military crisis of September 1862 came and the possible outcome of Civil War hung in the balance, Lincoln and Halleck went to McClellan's house and asked the general to take charge of the defeated, disorganized army of the Potomac which Lee had defeated in the second Battle of Bull Run. When Lincoln's friends expostulated with him because of his toleration of the man who had insulted him, he said, "Why, I would be willing to hold McClellan's horse, if only he will give victory to our army."

Was that weakness—or strength? It was the rugged strength of a man so big that he could completely subordinate all personal considerations to the welfare of the country he had sworn to defend. It represented the triumph of a soul who had fought and won bigger and more important conflicts than took place on the battlefields of the Civil War—the conflict of higher instincts over the lower, the battle of the soul with selfishness, false pride and egotism. That is what Jesus meant by "resist not evil." Weaklings cannot tolerate this principle. It takes real men and women who get their strength from on high.

The heroic, God-empowered, fearless personality of Jesus has inspired men to history's most outstanding deeds of selflessness for nineteen long centuries. From Rome comes the story of the forty wrestlers, Christian soldiers in one of the legions of the Roman army. The army was on a campaign in the high mountains of Armenia, in Asia Minor, and it was midwinter. The emperor had issued a decree that on a given day all soldiers must march past a statue of the emperor and worship him—do obeisance, pour out a libation of wine, and drop incense on the fire.

These forty Christians, however, could not do that and said so. The general loved them and pleaded with them to forget their Christ for only a few moments; otherwise, death on the frozen lake. For a moment they hesitated as they thought of the sweetness of life and their loved ones at home. Then they gave their answer: "We worship no one save our master, Jesus Christ."

Sadly the general ordered the penalty carried out. As the men were stripped naked, preparatory to driving them out onto the ice of a lake in the subzero cold, they were reminded that "only a little libation of wine, a bit of incense thrown on the fire and a small act of obeisance and you may live." But their minds were made up. Better death than the surrender of their consciences to evil.

Out into the freezing midnight cold they went singing, "Forty wrestlers wrestling for thee, O Christ, claim for thee the victory and from thee the crown."

As the night passed, their song grew fainter and fainter as man after man succumbed to the cold and fell lifeless on the ice. At length only one survivor was left. He appeared naked and trembling before the general's tent and agreed to pay homage to the emperor as God.

A sentinel nearby heard his cowardly recantation. "Since you have proved a coward," he said, "I will take your place." With that he stripped off his clothing and his armor and went out among the fallen men singing their song of the forty wrestlers until he too perished. When the morning sun rose over the bleak Armenian mountains, the members of one of Rome's legions saw the silent but brave witnesses of a Christ whose strength and love inspires men to give everything they have, once they have caught the contagion of his matchless personality.

That is the only personality that can match the terrible urgency of this dark hour. To a confused and despairing human race Jesus is the rugged personality with the secret of life who is still saying, "Follow me." Only by doing just that shall we save our civilization from the destruction that threatens it.

NIGHT OVER BETHLEHEM

It was night when Jesus was born. The shepherds kept watch over their flocks by night; the Wise Men eagerly followed a brilliant star by night; and in Herod's fearsome midnight councils, as their oil lamps threw weird shadows against the wall, evil men plotted the death of all the babes of Bethlehem. It was not only a dark time of the day, but it was a dark time in the lives of men.

But that is not the whole story. The star that guided the Wise Men to the baby Jesus was a meaningful symbol of the light that would henceforth shine into the remotest corner of this poor old world. A century later, the writer of the Fourth Gospel would be saying: "In him was life; and the life was the light of men." Jesus came into the world like the Sunburst of God and as Dr. Goodspeed renders it, "The light is still shining in the darkness, for the darkness has never put it out."

How deep is our gratitude for that fact. Only a few short years ago it still looked as though the Nazis, with their frank denial of every Christian virtue and their fervent belief in their ancient tribal gods, might conquer the world. That nightmare passed only to be replaced by the equally dread tyranny of Communism. But the moral universe of a just God will take care of that, too, in time.

All through the war that light was shining. A certain sailor had sat in a corner of the Boston Servicemen's Center most of the night looking lost and forlorn, only leaving his seat to enter his name every time there was a drawing for a free telephone call home. But he had no luck. One of the attendants noticed his gloom and learned that his name was Seaman Johnnie Quinn, that this was his first wedding anniversary and that he had not seen his bride for months and did not know when he would see her again. He had been hoping against hope that he might win a free telephone call to California and thus hear her voice once more before shipping out—perhaps forever.

The attendant hunted up the man in charge of the phone-call raffle and asked if it could not be "fixed" so Johnnie Quinn would win. The answer was flatly no—it would not be fair to the other men. A group of servicemen overheard the story and went off into a corner together, shaking their heads. Then a change of luck! On the very next drawing, Johnnie Quinn won and the glow on his face as he rushed into the telephone booth was really something! When the attendant was putting away the box that was used for drawing, he made a touching discovery. Every last one of the soldiers, sailors and marines that had overheard the story had written "Seaman Johnnie Quinn" on his card instead of his own name.

That typifies the very heart of the Christmas story—others-mindedness. "God so loved the world, that *he gave* his only begotten Son." And that Son's whole life was a luminous record of giving himself to frustrated, beaten men and women in the most selfless and loving spirit that has ever been manifested on this earth, drawing them irresistibly to the heavenly Father regardless of their race, color or creed. No wonder his birthday is a time of giving!

A Turkish woman not long ago made her way into a hospital in Ankara to watch a missionary doctor use his skill in the operating room. She observed the long lines of poor and diseased people awaiting their turn. She noted the doctor's solicitude for each one of them, even when he had worked so many hours he was ready to drop with fatigue. As he was leaving the hospital one evening, she boldly barred his way and started asking questions. Why did he come to Turkey? Did he have no job in his native Michigan? He told her that he had indeed had a very good job in Michigan; that he did miss the home folks very much; that he was receiving only a frugal living in Turkey

for twice the work he would have had to do at home. But he said
Christ had let a new light into his life that he was impelled to share
with others, and that he was happy helping to heal the diseased
bodies of strangers because they were God's children. He told her
that his Master had said, "Inasmuch as ye have done it unto one of
the least of these . . . ye have done it unto me." The woman looked
fixedly at the doctor for some time, as though overwhelmed with a
new vision of something too great for her. Then: "I've never known
very much about this Christ you mention, but if he is anything like
you, he must be wonderful. I'd like to know more about him."

A letter recently received from China tells this story:

I have been making trips north and south of Peking. In one chapel
I chanced upon a scene of over five hundred women and children
being served with porridge. It was one of the most moving sights I
have ever looked upon. Mothers and children sat in rows filling four
courtyards, and student volunteer workers passed up and down the
ranks filling the bowls. The faces of the people still showed traces of
the freezing temperatures they had endured, and I could not contem-
plate what they owed to the hot gruel in their struggle to exist
through those bitter nights. We feel thankful indeed to be used to
reclaim some of this human wreckage and direct them into hopeful
channels of life. It gives us an inexpressible joy to demonstrate even
in a small way the love of Christ for those stricken with despair.

The spirit of Christmas is as simple as the heart of a child. With
your gift you give yourself and your love without thought of personal
gain. The genuine article is not at all concerned with price tags. It is
concerned with heart beats. It is as elemental as the sun and the
wind and the rain, as the stars that gleamed over Galilee that holy
night in the long, long ago, and that still shine over an older, and we
dare hope, a wiser world.

In the Sandringham Church in Yorkshire, England, is one of the
most remarkable windows in the world. It was made out of broken
pieces of glass which had been thrown aside as worthless debris.
Love and reverence put them together, and when the sun shines
through, there is the complete picture of Christ. What a parable is
there at this Christmas season. The world lies in broken pieces and
millions of the sons of God feel as though fate had tossed them aside
on some rubbish heap. The only power on earth that can heal the

world's awful wounds is the ineffable spirit of Christ that is so much in evidence among us at Christmas time, but which must be made effective over increasing areas the whole year through.

In fact, this would be an excellent time to think things through along those very lines. Instead of allowing the spirit of competition and selfish commercialism to dominate us in 1952, with its power to kill the Christmas spirit and to lower the whole tone of life, why not determine now to live the spirit of Christmas through the coming year?

Volumes have been written about the spirit of self-giving that was manifested on every battlefield of the late war. Not long ago, President Truman presented the Medal of Honor to Private (first class) Desmond T. Doss at a White House ceremony. This highest military award which the American Government bestows went to a conscientious objector to war. The citation mentions six occasions when the youth exposed himself, unarmed, to enemy fire in efforts to aid wounded men, some of them occurring when he himself was severely wounded. Once, while lying on the ground badly shot up, he crawled off a little and insisted that another man take his place and be carried to safety. At Guam, Leyte and Okinawa, according to his commanding officer, his name became a symbol for outstanding gallantry.

One wonders what might happen to this poor suffering world if followers of the Master generally could be mobilized into a selfless army with banners to battle as valiantly in peace as in war! Christmas all year through! Every man starting where he was with what he had and going all out for the other fellow! How surprised we would be to find that some of the best work would be done by those who seemingly had the least to work with.

Take the case of a little girl in Cascadia, Washington. "The first time I took our little nine-year-old daughter out in her wheel chair without a robe over her lap," says her mother, "I was afraid that pitying glances at her crooked leg and twisted little hands would make her self-conscious. Instead, I noticed that more and more people were smiling cheerfully at her. A young girl winked at her and called out, 'Hello there, twerp.' A grave-faced sergeant grinned and gave her a snappy salute.

"When I lifted her out of the chair at the doctor's office, she explained the matter. 'I didn't want people to worry about me, so I kept smiling at them. I smiled extra big for the soldiers 'cause I think they are worried about going to war anyway.' "

The early Christians lived that way all through the year. Read the Apology of Aristides, discovered by Dr. Rendel Harris in the Syriac version on Mount Sinai in 1899, and addressed to Emperor Hadrian (117–138 A.D.) to whom it was dedicated:

They [the Christians] walk in all humility and kindness, and falsehood is not found among them. They love one another. They do not refuse to help widows. They rescue the orphan from violence. He who has gives ungrudgingly to him who lacks. If they see a stranger, they take him home and entertain him as a brother. . . . When one of their poor passes from this world, any one of them who sees it provides for his burial according to his ability. And if they hear that any one of their number is in prison or oppressed for the name of their Messiah, all of them provide for his needs. . . . Thus they labor to become righteous, as those who expect to see their Messiah and to receive from him the glorious fulfillment of the promises made to them. Truly this is a new people and there is something divine in them!

One wonders just what Hadrian thought of such a people. One thing is sure—the Roman Empire did not adopt and practice this way of life, and so they perished. And so shall we perish unless we practice the Christmas spirit right through the year. Gone is our geographical isolation; we are next-door neighbors to the rest of the world. Our arithmetic has become amazingly simplified. One is now the basic number: one world; one economy, that of plenty for all; one goal, to share life's obligations and life's benefits in order to attain the good life for all.

That is the real meaning of Christmas. Aristides' Apology informed the Roman Emperor Hadrian shortly after the turn of the first century that the Christians actually lived in that kind of a world. They were a light in the darkness. "The light is still shining in the darkness, for the darkness has never put it out." Shall we now let it flood the whole earth?

> Yet in thy dark streets shineth
> The everlasting light;
> The hopes and fears of all the years
> Are met in thee tonight.

THE VITALITY OF REMEMBERING

Nineteen years ago when little Dick came to live with us our cup of happiness was full to overflowing. Jim, Jon and Tom were six, four and two respectively and here was another fine little specimen of boyhood to make it a foursome. Seven weeks later, on a cold raw day in March, we said good-bye to little Dickie and returned home with benumbed hearts and minds. It was the first time that the Grim Reaper had invaded our home but we learned that he is no respecter of persons. The gland infection that swept through the children of the city that month was more than the little fellow could take.

I remember the effect of that leave-taking as though it were yesterday. Dickie's mother said to a few close friends: "No flowers, please; if you really want to do something, put the money into the unfolding life of some little fellow in a boys' home—some boy with no father or mother to love him." Our friends responded wholeheartedly to that thought so that quite a sum finally found its way into some little fellow's life in one of our boys' homes in the South. It has been a source of deep satisfaction ever since to know that some boy somewhere is better off; that something constructive found its way into another life because of Dick's death.

Although I was ill with the same infection and the doctor suggested that I stay out of the pulpit for two weeks, I could not do it. I felt under a divine compulsion to stand behind that sacred desk the very next Sunday and promise God in the presence of a multitude of witnesses that I would try to be a much better minister than I otherwise would have been had not Dickie left us. There are always so many dear people in need of sympathy and understanding and a helping hand. I felt I wanted Dick to live through my work. I have never forgotten and, unsatisfactory and incomplete as my ministry has been in many regards, I am sure it is better than it otherwise would have been.

When Charles Fletcher Lummis lost a beautiful lad of six, he wrote a chapter which he called "The Little Boy That Was." After giving the glowing heart's tribute of an unusual father, he writes: "It is good to remember; but *the vitality of remembering is to Do for its sake.*" It is one thing to have a flood tide of emotion tinted with the very light of heaven in memory of a recent loss that shakes the pattern of life to its foundations. It is quite another thing to realize that *the vitality of remembering is in doing something for somebody in need* and thus to register a permanent gain in the sum total of the world's good. Otherwise the force of the emotion becomes spent— and *irrevocably lost forever.*

Comes now this perfectly natural question: Why do some hearts respond constructively and hopefully to a death blow while others become cynical and bitter? The answer is that the hopeful ones have a vital faith in a good God. They know that God has a Son; that that Son died on a cross under conditions tragic and terrible enough to break any father's heart. Let no one think that the cross was not a terrific ordeal even for God. Jesus taught that God cares for even the least of his children far more than we can conceive; and, therefore, when they are hurt, His Heart is hurt also. He could take Good Friday, however, because He knew that Easter morning was coming; the event that would change the gloom of the tomb into a paean of joy and gladness forever. Every other son of God would thenceforth know that death is but the beginning of new life—and not death at all. Standing beside an open grave, the man of faith feels a tide of new strength and of high resolve come sweeping into his soul out of the ocean of God's love; he instinctively feels that the vitality of remembering is in doing something for somebody else and, behold, the death of a loved one results in a better world. God's will is done and we have the deep joy of knowing our loved one did not die in vain.

Soon after Dick's passing, that grand old man of Grinnell College, Dr. Edward A. Steiner, spent a day in our home. A week later the postman brought his little book, *My Doctor Dog,* inscribed: "To the loveliest mother of the dearest boys—from their admirer and friend." What a helpful friend he really was we did not fully grasp until we had read the book.

It is the story of Dr. Steiner's visit to a girls' school in New England: "a Dutch-New England-Irish-Scandinavian-Polish-Italian-Syrian and Lithuanian town; an ale-brewing, iron-molding, steel-casting, silk-weaving town" where there is also an elm-shaded campus where girls learn the fine art of living. It seems that Dr. Steiner casually mentioned to the girls that he had had a "doctor dog" as a small lad in his home in the Carpathian mountain country of Europe. So it was that this matchless story-teller spent a whole evening recounting the adventures of his little dog; a dog in a land where the peasants cherish the superstition that a friendly dog with "curative powers" may lick the face of a sick child and start him on the road to recovery.

Six-year-old Edward Steiner had such a dog. The village bully did not like the little terrier and their dislike was mutual. One time when this bully was about to display his great strength against an innocent bystander, the little dog, in spite of the fact that she was carrying quite a load of unborn puppies, attacked the bully and ripped off quite a piece of his trousers. Unable to get away fast enough, the doctor dog received the bully's boot in the pit of her stomach and, the next day, this brave little friend of childhood died.

Evelyn Kew, a senior girl from a well-to-do family, remained after the others had gone asking Dr. Steiner all manner of questions about immigrant women and what could and should be done for them in just such a situation as confronted them in that very town. Before she finally said good night, she said in a tearful voice: "God helping me, there will be another chapter to the story of your doctor dog."

But Evelyn Kew did not *do* anything—not for a long, long time. She married a wealthy young man who rose to high position among the executives of one of the great factories in the town; but the camp with the fresh air and wholesome food and loads of fun she had talked of for the workers' undernourished children was forgotten.

The years sped by and then, one day, Dr. Steiner received a black-embroidered letter from Evelyn Kew Prescott. It is so remarkable that I reproduce it in full:

My Dear Friend:

I am asking you to come to us again and at once, if possible, for we sorely need you. I know you will come, although you will find our home desolate.

A few weeks ago we entertained a guest who came unbidden and unwelcome, and departed as quickly as he came, taking with him our precious Dorothy and leaving us heart-broken.

I would have telegraphed you to come then when we most needed your help; for I knew you would say the words we ought to hear— but I dared not. I must confess to you that I was afraid to have you come. With the thought of you and the words you would say, came from far away the remembrance of my college days and the high purposes which then filled my soul. Something dead and buried had its resurrection, and the thought of that something hurts almost more than the loss of our dear darling.

I was afraid that your mere presence would remind me that I had broken my promise, that I had been false to my better self, that I had killed, or lived down, the high purposes which, years ago, you had aroused.

I proved coward and permitted an almost perfect stranger (I am ashamed to say that we have had no church home) to read the burial service in a perfunctory way and say words which scarcely reached my ears, much less my benumbed heart.

Every day since then, I have accused myself of cowardice, and now an inner compulsion forces me to ask you to come to us. Please do not delay; for in some way this pain must become a blessing! I know it will. My very desolation seems to be changing into a Presence which I fear will leave me unless I realize my desire, and then I shall be desolate indeed.

We were so cruelly unprepared for the blow. A slight fever seemed the only trouble. The doctor and a nurse came and I felt secure. Then more doctors and more nurses, and then the great desolation!

Just as mother love came with the great agony of bringing my darling into the world, it came again with the agony of seeing her go out of it. I don't want to lose that love! Oh, do come and help me!

I have determined that this solemn, holy feeling must not leave me, and I don't know how to keep it unless I do something, create something, to hold it fast; something big enough and costly enough and useful enough to express the love I now feel, not only for my child, but for all children.

I am realizing for the first time what mother love really means, and I don't want ever to forget.

Let me tell you what I am planning, for you must help me work it out. I want that camp, which I have so cruelly neglected, to be Dorothy's own, all of it. It is selfish, I know; but pain is always selfish. I feel my life very small and centered around my dead child who must live and live always.

I want the camp to have just such a nursery as Dorothy had; only it must be large enough for all the children who need it. I wish I could release all the mothers from our factory. Mr. Prescott would gladly do it for my sake; but we are both powerless. The directors and stockholders cannot share that great look into human misery which our sorrow had brought us.

It's a wild sort of plan I have; bigger and better than I can put on paper, but I have money enough to carry it out. Do come while my heart is warm with grief, and I am ready to do anything and everything; for I fear it will not last. I know my nature too well. My husband is as anxious as I am that you should help us; so do not hesitate, but come at once, please.

Faithfully yours,

EVELYN KEW PRESCOTT

So it happened that, in the course of time, a wonderful summer camp was opened for the children of the whole town. Dr. Steiner was the orator of the day. He tells us: "I experienced that great mystery of being blended with human hearts, and so felt my oneness with them all; but I reached a higher level than I ever reached before— I had a glimpse of another world. I saw a plot of blue grass (there must be blue grass in Heaven) and a dear little girl, playing with a dog. I knew it was my dog. . . ." And on that same day Evelyn Kew Prescott learned by experience that *the vitality of remembering is in doing something for somebody who is in need.*

While I was the pastor of the Congregational Church in West Lebanon, New Hampshire, I drove up to Dartmouth four miles away to see the beautiful memorial dormitory built by Mr. and Mrs. Hall in memory of Dick Hall. He was an unusually fine lad who had been cut off suddenly in his freshman year. As I entered the building I was greeted by the smiling, genial parents who had adopted every boy who was living in this beautiful dormitory. "This is the way Dick would have wanted it," they said.

At the far side of the spacious library was a beautiful Chime Clock ringing merrily every quarter hour. Inside was this inscription written by Boyd Edwards, principal of the Hill School where Dick had prepared for college: "Sometimes I think of a young life like this falling silent and yet it does not fall silent—there is a music from it forever. After all, it does not make much difference how many times the bell in some beautiful chime tower sounds out but all the difference in the world is made by the tone of that bell for as long as it does sound. The tone of Dick's life was clear and sweet and beautiful. It will sound in the hearts of those who knew him as long as memory lasts and that makes his meaning and message abide as a lovely inspiring thing."

Mr. and Mrs. Hall were finding that the vitality of remembering Dick lay in serving countless numbers of other boys at Dartmouth.

They did not delay until their beautiful impulse had faded and died as do so many of us. Every minister has had the experience of talking with bereaved members of a family who have lost some loved one to the Grim Reaper. Their hearts have been soft and tender and responsive. They have put themselves on record as being determined to live more worthily by doing this or that. Then, as the days have come and gone, the old life pattern of self-centeredness has gradually reasserted itself and the beautiful impulse has faded and died. Procrastination is the thief of time—and we mean *thief!*

The story is told of a man who dreamed one night that he was carried to a conference of evil spirits. They were discussing the best means of destroying men. One rose and said, "I will go to earth and tell them the Bible is a fable, and not God's word." Another said, "Persuade them that Christ was only a man." Still another said, "Let me go; I will tell them there is no God, no Savior, no heaven." "No, that will not do," they said. "We could never make men believe that." Finally one old devil, wise as a serpent but not as harmless as a dove, rose and said, "Let me go; I will journey to the world of men and tell them that there is a God, there is a Savior, there is a heaven. But I will tell them there is no hurry; tomorrow will do; tomorrow will be even as today!" And he was the devil they sent!

THE SOUL'S LISTENING POST

The great broadcasting chains all maintain "listening posts" where certain individuals make it their main business to listen in on foreign broadcasts and faithfully record what is heard. In some such sense every soul should have a "listening post," manned at least a little time each day in order to learn something, at first hand, of what God is trying to say to us. The trouble with most of us is that we become so thoroughly consumed with the broadcasting side of life that we forget all about the listening post. That is why a very great deal of what we give the world is simply not worth the taking. Our intake does not keep pace with our outgo. The result is disaster. The chaotic condition of the world at this moment is an eloquent testimony of that fact.

Arthur Farwell in the magazine *Tomorrow* for April, 1942, tells of some interesting results of the listening attitude in his own life. Mr. Farwell has been Supervisor of Municipal Music in New York City, lecturer on music at Cornell University and head of the Music Department at the University of California. It was his community music work at Santa Barbara that inspired the financing and building of the Hollywood Bowl. For twelve years he was also head of the department of Theory of Music at the University of Michigan while he continued writing music. He tells us that in 1913 he agreed to compose the music for a whole series of pageant dramas. He did not have the time to do it in the ordinary way—that of waiting for a mood and then straining for musical ideas. Instead, he conceived that the Universal Mind contained all the musical ideas which had ever been thought of and written down. He imagined a great place of music where everything musical was to be had; a universal orchestra and chorus of immense proportions. "Then I set this musical mass equipment in my mind, in a semi-distant misty dreamspot, far enough away to be free of any interference from myself. As definitely as possible I then thought of the particular kind of theme I needed for a certain scene in the drama on which I was working. *I watched the musical equipment of the universal store intently out of a dreamy state of my own, with closed eyes,* keeping out of my mind every thought except the one on which I had concentrated. It required only a moment before the appropriate theme spoke out from the appropriate instrument or instruments, apparently wholly by its own volition, and absolutely *without any effort of composition on my part.* At once I found myself spontaneously released from the dreamstate, and went to work in the ordinary way, developing the theme which the 'Universe' had so promptly and generously given me. This process I repeated for months, obtaining immediately and in rapid succession the themes I required, which always fitted precisely my expressed need."

Mr. Farwell goes on to tell us that he used this technique for twenty years, thinking that it would work for him only in the musical field. Then he found himself face to face with a life-situation problem —one involving some human relationships wellnigh intolerable and for which he could find no solution. He then used the same technique and was given a definite answer quite contrary to what his reason had deduced. He followed the direction of the deeper intuition and found it was the true answer. "It made me realize that the solution of reason-baffling problems *in any field or direction of thought* could be obtained by this same procedure."

Mr. Farwell then states the three matters of prime importance. (1) The question must rise from a genuine and vital need of progress, growth or existence on the part of the questioner, which his reason cannot solve for him. (2) The question must be defined with the utmost clarity and sharpness, and asked of the hidden Mind in oneself (The Kingdom of Heaven is within you!) with faith that the answer will be given sooner or later. . . . (3) Occasions of quiet receptiveness should be provided for the receiving of such an intuition. It is, above all, necessary to realize that we have an Answering Intelligence within or accessible to us, of illimitable reach and irrefrageable authority. It is necessarily Mind, but one which the ordinary waking mind cannot consciously perceive, except in the intuitive flash itself. Between this Answering Intelligence and our conscious minds is a veil, but not a sound-proof and light-proof wall. The height and magnitude of the intuitive answers which we receive from this inner and superior Mind *will be in accordance with the height and magnitude which we ascribe to it.* This is a profound matter of mental and spiritual growth.

Let us note well these conditions. There must be a deep felt *need*. Jesus put it bluntly one day when he said that pearls are never cast before swine. The swine would not appreciate them. The wisdom of God is never given to any soul until enough mistakes have been made to cause our troubled and baffled souls to cry out to Someone stronger than we are for help. The need must be deeply felt. Then we must have *faith* that the answer will come. "Therefore I say unto you, What things soever ye desire, when ye pray, believe that ye receive them, and ye shall have them." (Mark 11:24) The time to do this is on "occasions of quiet receptiveness." We are to "be still—and know that I am God." Jesus had good reason to spend many a quiet hour on some lonely mountain height listening to God. It always paid rich dividends.

Well, there is the testimony of one of the great, creative, musical artists of America. He believes that as we grow spiritually and develop definite techniques for doing so, that we can tap almost unlimited storehouses of power. George Washington Carver astounded the scientists of the world with his amazing discoveries. He practiced the Farwell technique in his own simple way and got even more remarkable results. The entire nation has benefited from his work. Down in the depths of personality is a meeting place where God can be found—a well of living water springing up unto everlasting life.

The Quakers have always been firm believers in a listening post for the soul. They call it the "guidance of the inner light." It is a matter of deep significance that the Society of Friends, or Quakers, have the highest reputation in the world for selfless service in the distribution of aid to the needy. In the midst of the noise and confusion of our modern world, groups of Friends still meet in their plain little churches and wait in the silence for the voice and guidance of God. Their vast contribution to America's development from the beginning would seem to show how often they get that guidance.

One of the greatest of the early Quakers, William Penn, was born on October 24, 1644. The world in general and America in particular owe him more than we have realized. Jefferson is credited with having given us the Declaration of Independence with its clarion and Christian insistence upon the infinite worth of the common man. *"We hold these truths to be self-evident: that all men are created equal; that they are endowed by their Creator with certain inalienable rights; that among these are life, liberty and the pursuit of happiness."* Jefferson wrote those immortal words but he was profoundly influenced by Penn who, he says, "was the greatest lawyer who ever lived." Born into a family of wealth and social standing, he was nevertheless to spend his life fighting for equality, tolerance, justice and decency.

His great fights for civil rights and religious freedom were fought in England where he was thrown into jail four times for speaking or writing as a Quaker. His most famous trial in 1670, on a charge of causing a riot by preaching in Gracechurch Street, is a landmark in English history. Penn was acquitted but the court was incensed by the fact that this young upstart knew so much law that he successfully argued his own case. So they sent Penn and the entire jury to jail anyway! The jurors appealed and after two years won the case that was to establish a right that has ever since been cherished by English and American citizens alike—the right to free and unbossed juries.

It turned out to be a blessing to the world that Charles II owed

Penn's father sixteen thousand pounds which he could not pay. Thus it eventually came about that William Penn was given Pennsylvania in lieu of the debt. Here, in 1682, he made his famous treaty with chief Tammany. Voltaire said that this treaty was the only one in history that was made without oath and the only one that was never broken. Penn believed that justice and brotherly love and human decency should be one's guiding principles in dealing with all men, regardless of the color of their skins. He believed all men to be sons of God and that they should therefore be treated as such. The Indians had an intense affection for him and he never had any trouble with them as long as he lived.

See what happened, however, after he died. Penn arranged the famous "Walking Purchase" by which he bought from the Indians all the land north along the Delaware River that a man could cover in a three-day walk. He himself walked off a day and a half of the purchase in leisurely fashion. In 1737, long after his death, Governor Thomas Penn, his son, hired three famous backwoodsmen to complete the purchase. The fastest of them ran—not walked—more than sixty miles in thirty-six hours, defrauding the Indians of valuable hunting grounds. This led to wars on the Pennsylvania frontier which did not end until the Indians were virtually exterminated.

Herein lies a truth that must not escape us in this critical hour. When Penn actually put Brotherly Love and Justice into his promises and treaties and lived up to this high standard there was peace and harmony. When, on December 7, 1682, his followers passed the "Great Law of Pennsylvania" whereby Pennsylvania was to become a Christian State based on the Quaker model, they were following the advice of one of the most practical men who ever lived. Christianity works. It is practical hard-headed realism as well as Godlike idealism. But when greed and avarice entered the picture fifty years later; when justice was replaced by selfishness and the Indians defrauded of their land, then the hatreds of men produced the inevitable bloodshed and chaos. When shall we learn to accept this eternal truth?

Penn's insight was God-given. At the age of twelve he was "suddenly surprised with an inward comfort and, as he thought, an external glory in the room, which gave rise to religious emotions, during which he had the strongest conviction of the being of God, and that the soul of man was capable of enjoying communication with him."

He became a Quaker and *counseled men to seek and to follow the Inner Light at all costs.* He himself paid a high price, for religious toleration and freedom were then unknown. He was "banished" from college and whipped and beaten by his father and turned out of doors, but the inner light continued to shine. Four times he went to prison and each time used his enforced leisure to write pamphlets and books in defense of his faith. That is the man whose priceless contributions of religious freedom and democratic self-government, based on equality and justice and brotherly love, were written into the Declaration of Independence and the Constitution of the United States! What a heritage! What results from Penn's listening post!

Dr. Elwood Worcester in his great book, *Body, Mind and Spirit,* tells us that there was a creative period of his life that lasted about five years when many of his best sermons were given him from the Infinite Storehouse. "Once, in the time it took to pass from my dining room up a flight of stairs to my study, two complete discourses were given to me of which it was necessary only to jot down the outlines so that I should not forget them. During the first days of the week I would frequently hear a text spoken as if by another person, and I would repeat it to my wife and say, 'That must be the text of my next sermon.' When I sat down to write, often it was exactly as if a superior and more facile mind were near me, dictating thoughts and words more rapidly than I could record them on paper."[1] Dr. Worcester was for twenty-five years pastor of the Emmanuel Episcopal Church of Boston. Twenty-five thousand troubled people passed through his Spiritual Clinic during those years and most of them received the spiritual guidance that helped them to tie their lives in with God in a way that led them to victory over life's bafflements.

Jesus once told his disciples that after he was gone they would find themselves in trouble before Sanhedrins and Synagogues and they "will deliver you up to the councils." Then he added: "But when they deliver you up, take no thought how or what ye shall speak: for it shall be given you in that same hour what ye shall speak. For it is not ye that speak, but the Spirit of your Father which speaketh in you."

---

[1] Reprinted from *Body, Mind and Spirit* by Elwood Worcester and Samuel McComb; copyright 1931 by Charles Scribner's Sons; used by permission of the publishers.

(Matthew 10:19, 20) Jesus believed that a relaxed and confident faith in God would release heavenly wisdom at critical moments.

What might come about if the bumbling statesmen of the world should establish a listening post in order daily to catch the Voice of the Eternal? And what might happen to you and me were we to practice listening intently to the Still Small Voice every day of our lives? In the Universal Storehouse of God is all the wisdom that any of us needs for the building of the good life for all. In that storehouse is the complete plan for the establishment of a peaceful world full of wholesome people. Will we listen?

 ## EMPOWERED BY FAITH

Channing Pollock tells us that he and Basil King were sitting together in a restaurant one day when they overheard a woman at the next table say to her companion, "It's a disgraceful state of affairs, but what can one man do?" The author of *The Conquest of Fear* looked at Pollock for a moment and then asked, "Shall we tell her that everything of importance in the world was begun by one man—or one woman?"

What can one man do? Who has not asked himself that question? In these days of possible mass destruction and wholesale death when the man of ideals feels so helpless in the face of titanic demonic powers we are reminded of Mrs. Partington's great fight with the Atlantic Ocean in 1824. In the midst of a terrible storm, Mrs. Partington, who occupied a cottage on the beach, was seen trundling her mop, squeezing out sea water and vigorously pushing back the Atlantic Ocean. Sydney Smith wrote that "The Atlantic was aroused; Mrs. Partington's spirit was up; but I need not tell you that the contest was unequal. The Atlantic Ocean beat Mrs. Partington."

Yes, we tend to feel like that sometimes but let us not carry the illustration too far. The forces of evil are not the Atlantic Ocean in comparison with the forces of righteousness seen in a Partington mop. No, sir! Quite the contrary. Read the eleventh chapter of Hebrews (Weymouth translation) on faith: *"Now faith is a well-grounded assurance of that for which we hope, and a conviction of the reality of things which we cannot see. For by it the saints of old won God's* approval. Through faith we understand that the worlds came into being, and still exist, at the command of God, so that what is seen does not owe its existence to that which is visible." (vs. 1–3)[1]

We had better stop there a moment for this is sheer, naked, unadulterated power with which we are dealing. The creation of the world and everything in it was accomplished by an act of faith of the Divine Mind. Before there was any visible thing in the universe there was a pattern of it all in the Infinite Mind and the belief that that pattern would come into materialization. That is the power that underlies creation. *God Himself does His work through faith!*

"That's all right for God," I hear someone say, "but we poor humans aren't God." No, my friend, you are not God, but you are made in God's spiritual image and *we can be creators together with God if we have His brand of creative faith.* Come on down to the sixth verse now: "But where there is no faith it is impossible truly to please Him; for the man who draws near to God must believe that there is a God and that He proves Himself a rewarder of those who earnestly try to find Him."

Then comes the roll call of the men of old who had faith: "Through faith Abraham, upon being called to leave home and go into a land which he was soon to receive for an inheritance, obeyed: and *he went out, not knowing where he was going.*" (vs. 8)[1] I am glad those words are there: "not knowing where he was going." The way is dark and so poorly marked for such long stretches that we need to know of others who finally arrived over an uncharted way. "Through faith Moses, when he grew to manhood, refused to be known as Pharaoh's daughter's son, having determined to endure ill treatment along with the people of God rather than enjoy the short-lived pleasures of sin; because he deemed the reproaches which he might meet with to be greater riches than all the treasures of Egypt; for he fixed his gaze on the coming reward. Through faith he left Egypt, not being frightened by the king's anger; *for he held on his course* as seeing the unseen One." (vs. 24–27)[1]

On and on it runs with an ever-mounting crescendo until our unknown author cries: "Therefore, surrounded as we are by such a vast cloud of witnesses let us fling aside every encumbrance and the sin

---

[1] *Weymouth's New Testament in Modern Speech.* Published by Harper & Brothers. Used by permission.

that so readily entangles our feet. And let us run with patient endurance the race that lies before us, simply fixing our gaze upon Jesus, our Prince Leader in the faith. . . . He, for the sake of the joy which lay before Him, patiently endured the cross, looking with contempt upon its shame. . . . Therefore if you would escape becoming weary and faint-hearted, compare your own sufferings with those of Him. . . ." (12:1–3)[2] That is great reading for days like these when it is so easy to become pessimistic and to lose our faith in God and man. Nothing worthwhile has ever come at a low price.

William Lloyd Garrison was born when human slavery was still regarded as a divine institution by most of his countrymen. When he died it had been banished as a legalized institution from the civilized world. When someone praised Lincoln for freeing the slaves, he spoke feelingly of "the logic and moral power of Garrison" as largely responsible. This amazing man caught a vision of slavery for the horrible human injustice that it really was. He believed in a God who would crush it once and forever if He could find human helpers through whom He could work. Garrison gave himself body and soul to that dream.

When he launched the *Liberator* he had no capital and no subscribers. The type for the first issue was borrowed and then some secondhand type was secured from a foundry. The paper was printed by a hand press. Garrison and his partner, Isaac Knapp, lived in the printing office, sleeping on the floor and securing their meager food from a near-by bakery. They gathered their news, wrote it up, set it into type, ran it off and then delivered their own fiery product. For thirty-five years Garrison was the editor of the *Liberator* and during all that time he never for one moment forgot the crusading words that he wrote for his first issue on January 1, 1831:

I will be as harsh as truth, and as uncompromising as justice. On this subject I do not wish to think, or speak, or write with moderation. No! No! Tell a man whose house is on fire to give a moderate alarm; tell him to moderately rescue his wife from the hands of a ravisher; tell the mother to gradually extricate her babe from the fire into which it has fallen;—but urge me not to use moderation in a cause like the present. I am in earnest—I will not equivocate—I will not excuse—I will not retreat a single inch—and I will be heard.

2 *Weymouth's New Testament in Modern Speech.* Published by Harper & Brothers. Used by permission.

That man believed in something with all of his heart and mind. He could be dragged through the streets of Boston with a rope around his neck but he could not be silenced. John Jay Chapman has put it in the following remarkable paragraph:

It was between 1830 and 1840 that the real work of Garrison was done. At the beginning of that decade abolition was a cry in the wilderness: at the end of it abolition was a part of the American mind. . . . It was Garrison who caused the heat-lightning of 1824 to turn into the thunderbolts of 1835. We must imagine Garrison then, as always, behind and underneath the machinery and in touch with all the forces at work, writing away at his terrible Liberator—fomenting, rebuking, retorting, supporting, expounding, thundering, scolding. The continuousness of Garrison is appalling, and fatigues even the retrospective imagination of posterity: he is like something let loose. I dread the din of him. I cover my head and fix my mind on other things; but there is Garrison hammering away, till he catches my eye and forces me to attend to him. If Garrison can do this to me, who am protected from the dread of him by eighty years of intervening time, think how his lash must have fallen upon the thin skins of our ancestors.

Yes, Garrison was terrific; but I can hear many mild Christian friends saying that "he must have been a very unlovely eccentric, and who wants to be like that?" On the contrary, Garrison was not that way at all. A friend who spent several weeks with the Garrisons in Europe wrote: "As to Mr. Garrison himself, he is the most delightful man I have ever known—magnanimous, generous, considerate, and, as far as I can see, every way morally excellent." Wendell Phillips wrote: "I have seen him intimately for thirty years. . . . I never saw him unhappy. I never saw the moment that serene abounding faith in the rectitude of his motive, the soundness of his method, and the certainty of success did not lift him above all possibility of being reached by any clamor about him." Oliver Johnson, his lifelong friend, said that Garrison had "a faith so absolute in the sacredness and power of moral principles, a trust in God so firm and immovable as I have never seen exhibited by any other man."

That is all God is waiting for; just an ever-growing number of people who have that kind of faith. It is creative, it sweeps everything before it. War will be banished from the earth by that kind of faith one day. It will not come about through mild debating societies of the "both and," "either or" variety. No, a few Garrisons will one day appear with a faith that will remove this mountain from the face of the earth forever.

Did you see what happened in Colorado some time ago? Caught up in a brief fury of anti-Japanese excitement, stimulated by a vitriolic campaign in the Denver *Post,* Governor Vivian of Colorado called a special session of the legislature to approve and submit a constitutional amendment which would make it impossible for any Japanese, American or otherwise, to own land in the state. They did not want the twelve hundred Japanese from the Pacific coast who had been resettled in Colorado to stay. All was going well for this bit of un-American procedure until Sergeant Hill took the stand. This twenty-six-year-old discharged soldier lashed out with deep conviction against the bill on the ground of unfair racial discrimination. Hurriedly the boys got him off in a corner and warned him that such an unpopular stand would ruin his career in politics forever. His reply was a masterpiece: "I am just as willing to die a political death as I am to die in battle to preserve American freedom." After that the campaign for the amendment sputtered and went out like a wet fuse. The house voted 60 to 1 against even appointing a committee to study the problem. One man with vision, with conviction and with faith can confound a multitude.

How Garrison would have thrilled could he have known the story of one of the slaves he helped to free. Talk about the power of faith! Booker T. Washington could not remember having slept in a bed until his family was freed by the Emancipation Proclamation. He slept on a pile of rags in a corner of the log cabin. One day, while at work in a coal mine, this small black boy overheard some talk about Hampton Institute, a school for Negroes. The place seemed like a corner of heaven and he dreamed of it day and night. Finally the great day came and off he started for Hampton on foot, a distance of five hundred miles. On reaching Richmond, he did not have a penny, so he slept under a sidewalk on the ground for several nights.

Finally this black boy with the unfulfilled vision arrived at Hampton Institute. He had been without food, without bathing facilities or clean clothes so long that he was in despair lest they refuse to let him in. During the hard gruelling years that followed, Booker T. Washington grew into a truly great soul with a still bigger dream— the dream of a greater school than Hampton somewhere in the deep south where he could fit countless numbers of other Negro folks for the business of lifting the whole Negro race.

Today the entire world knows of Tuskegee. Twenty years after beginning in a broken-down shanty and an old hen-house, Mr. Washington had built an institution of 66 buildings on 2,300 acres of land. The property and endowment were valued at $1,700,000. The number of students had grown from 30 to 1,400 drawn from 27 states. He had disproved the assertion that the Negro was essentially inferior by building up and conducting an institution almost as large as Yale without a single white man being connected with the place.

Faith! Vision! Courage! These things are creative if a man can but keep on keeping on nor ever lose his grip. This Negro was so unselfconscious and so lost in his work that he was equally at home having lunch with Theodore Roosevelt in the White House, at Windsor Castle with Queen Victoria or with his Negro neighbors in the south.

John Kendrick Bangs once wrote a poem that we could all read with profit when the flame of life burns low and faith in our ability to continue the struggle is all but dead. As you read this poem note how the man is prepared to eliminate one advantage after another without giving way to discouragement:

> If there's no sun I still can have the moon;
> If there's no moon the stars my needs suffice;
>   Or if these fail I have my evening lamp;
> Or, lampless, there's my trusty tallow dip,
> And if the dip goes out, my couch remains
> Where I may sleep, and dream there's light again.[3]

FEAR AND FAITH

Let me tell you a true story. When a wealthy New York business man, Joseph Stanley, lost everything in the stock-market crash of 1929, he went to pieces. Friends who had weathered the storm offered to back him with a good loan but he said he was through. He repeated that he was physically and mentally ill and not to be trusted with other people's money.

3 Published by George Sully Company of New York in *Silver Lining,* p. 78.

His charming wife, Alice, had a thousand dollars in her savings account and with that she took him to a quiet lake in Florida where they were surrounded by Florida "Crackers." There Mr. Stanley would sit on the bank by the hour staring into the placid water. He could not sleep and he could not eat. He kept repeating to himself that he was a failure and all done. His basic security, which had been money, was gone.

One day on the way back to the cottage he saw a big boy beating a smaller lad and in trying to stop the fight he pushed the bigger one into a tree so hard it cut his face. Shaking his fist in baffled rage the big boy vowed that his pa would settle Mr. Stanley's hash in short order.

That evening our young ruffian returned to the Stanley cottage to say that his pa would be over the next morning and that Mr. Stanley had better get out of town or he would be shot. A neighbor came to say that Jed Colby, half drunk, had been down to the village telling his cronies that "no dang 'furriner' could draw blood on his boy without paying with his life."

He arose quietly at 4:00 A.M. and started for Jed Colby's home. He would walk straight into the jaws of death and die facing his enemy. Strangely enough, as he walked along the road on his grim errand he was no longer afraid. God suddenly seemed friendly and close and real to him. The sunrise looked beautiful as the golden disk appeared over the Everglades.

He knocked on Jed Colby's door and presently was confronted by the bad man himself, rifle in hand. Stanley was smiling and unafraid. "I'm not armed," he said. "You can go ahead and shoot me at your pleasure but before you do I'd like to have a little talk with you." Jed Colby put down his gun. "I can't shoot an unarmed man on my doorstep," he said, "especially not a brave man like you."

When Mr. Stanley arrived back at his little cottage his wife was waiting for him with tears in her eyes and arms outstretched. "I knew when you went," she said, "and I also knew you had to go. So I lay very still and prayed. After a short while a great peace enveloped me and I knew you had found yourself again." And sure enough he had.

Joseph Stanley had conquered fear by doing several things. *He accepted the situation as it was* and *went out to face it* even if it meant his death. He resolved never to run away from trouble again but to confront it with faith in God and in himself. In so doing a magic balm took possession of his fearful heart and the trouble evaporated into thin air.

That is the formula for overcoming any fear. (1) Face it. Walk straight toward the thing you fear even if it means death. (2) Turn the stream of consciousness away from self toward God and man in the confidence that the strength of God is your strength and that the world of mankind is basically friendly. The result will be victory.

I know this to be true from personal experience. At least ten years of my life were years of black torment from fear of people. I could not recite in class without knocking knees and shaking voice in grade school, high school and through two years of college. When I went out to sell the Volume Library between high school and college I alternated between success and abysmal failure. In some towns I could not sell a single book because of my fear of the simple housewives to whom I must give my "canvass" talk.

Fear builds prison walls around a man and bars him in with dreads, anxieties, and timid doubts. Faith is the great liberator from prison walls. Fear paralyzes, faith empowers; fear disheartens, faith encourages; fear sickens, faith heals; fear puts hopelessness at the heart of life while faith sees beyond the horizon and rejoices in its God.

At this point I can hear some fear-dazed soul saying: "I agree with all you say but I still keep on with the old treadmill of fear, getting precisely nowhere with my fine resolves to break loose." Mark this then, my friend: The way to begin the hopeful Faith-Way-of-Life is to begin—now. As Andrew Jackson said about the difficulty of resuming specie payments in the bank: "The way to resume is to resume." Thinking about this vital matter is a prerequisite but it is not enough; we must step boldly forth and start *acting as though God does care and does empower us.* Listen to this word of wisdom: "But he that doeth the truth cometh to the light." (John 3:21) It is men of *action* that come to know the truth.

When I arrived in Buchanan, Michigan, to sell the Volume Library I had been acting like a bum for a week and I had a bum's mental outlook for the time being—that of failure. In my memory was the night in Louisville when, with a dime apiece in our pockets, Whitney and I entered a cheap-looking restaurant down by the tracks and found ourselves in the back end of a saloon. We chose crackers and milk, knowing we would get one bowl of milk for our dime, but speculating that the waitress would set out a big bowl of crackers which we planned to demolish completely. She set them out all right but (whether she sensed our plan or not I do not know) she took them away again as soon as we had one helping!

Another thing that was in my mind as I entered Buchanan was an experience on the freight train a hundred miles or so out of Cincinnati. I had crawled into a long three-foot drainage tile that ran the length of a flat car. Thinking I was safe from detection I had gone to sleep and was dreaming about home and mother when a harsh voice yelled, "Hey you blankety blank so and so, come out of there!" Awakening from my pleasant dream, I looked toward the end of the tile ten feet away and there, silhouetted against the sunlight, was the face of a brakeman who had been hunting me unsuccessfully all the night before. I shall never forget his scorn when he learned I did not have the dollar bribe which he was after as a concession to letting us stay on the train.

As I walked up the tracks in Buchanan with a ticket for Niles in my pocket, I went over the last hideous month. I knew I had carried the atmosphere and outlook of failure into this little town with me. I had not acted for one hour as though I expected to sell a book. As I walked I prayed.

Suddenly I made up my mind. I would go into Niles *believing* I could get back into the groove and plaster the place full of my excellent product; and I would act as though I believed it from the first contact. At that moment the train appeared around the bend. It now looked different to me. Faith had replaced fear and so even the engine smoke rolled heavenward with a jaunty air. In Niles the man of faith became the man of action. The bum's mentality was jettisoned forever. One sale led to another and before we left Niles, enough of our fine books had been sold to raise the intellectual level of the whole town! Best of all, my Christian faith had been greatly strengthened. I had proved once again that when a man puts his faith to the test and dares to step right out in a field of action just as though fear was not there, that fear disappears.

Basil King in his *Conquest of Fear* gave the world one of the best

guides for the overcoming of demon fear that has ever been written.
He was going blind. As an author, dependent upon voluminous reading, this meant the probable end of his career. Furthermore he was
at odds with his publishers and unable to get his product published.
He tells us that he sat in the lonely gardens of Versailles one fall
amid falling leaves and empty palaces thinking the whole problem
through. He was afraid of the future. Gradually he worked out a
three point basis for the conquest of his fear.

1. This is God's world. He made it and me and I am his agent. He
is my Father all-sufficient, all-good. He is Spirit, Love and Light. A
verse of scripture leaped into new life and significance: "Trust in the
Lord and do good and verily thou shalt be fed. Delight thyself in the
Lord and he shall give thee the desires of thy heart."

2. All other men are also his children and his agents, including my
publishers and I should see them thus.

3. These two things being true, all suspicion and fear must go. I
must live *now* as a good son dwelling in the Father's home. For "God
is our refuge and strength, a very present help in trouble. Therefore
will we *not fear*, though the earth be removed and though the mountains be carried into the midst of the sea."

Basil King started acting *as if* this was all true. The man of faith
became the man of action. He faced the thing he feared with confidence and went forward. He tells us that his blind condition was
healed and the difficulty with his publishers evaporated into thin air
and that his fear was gone forever.

The important thing then, in dealing with fear, is to stand up and
face it and defy it with faith in the power of Almighty God to overcome it then and there or die in the process. Certain it is that running
away from it will never bring a solution.

Abraham Lincoln had a step-brother who was lazy and who kept
himself poor moving from place to place because he always thought
opportunities for advancement would be greater elsewhere. When
Lincoln heard he was about to sacrifice his farm in Illinois and move
to Missouri, Lincoln wrote him this wise letter:

What can you do in Missouri better than here? Is the land any
richer? Can you there, any more than here, raise corn and wheat and
oats without work? Will anybody there, any more than here, do the
work for you? If you intend to go to work, there is no better place
than right where you are; if you do not intend to go to work, you

cannot get along anywhere. Squirming and crawling about from place to place can do you no good.

And so it is with fear of any and every variety. Squirming and crawling about from place to place can do us no good. So why not take a stand here and now, and, looking at the fiendish thing, fight it through to a finish?

Preston Bradley tells of sitting beside a dying cowboy, "Tell me what important thing you have learned from experience that stands out in your memory at this solemn hour," said Dr. Bradley softly. After a few moments of silence the cowboy replied:

"The Herefords taught me one of life's most important lessons. We used to breed cattle for a living but the severe winter storms used to take an awful toll. Again and again after a severe winter storm we would find most of them piled up against fences dead. They would turn their backs to the icy blasts and slowly drift down-wind twenty miles until the fence stopped them. There they piled up and died.

"But the Herefords were different. They would head straight into the wind and slowly work up the other way until they came to our upper boundary fence where they still stood facing into the storm. We always found them alive and well. That's the greatest lesson I ever learned on these Western prairies."

TRY THIS FOR ONE WEEK

Modern science agrees with the Bible in affirming that our universe has been created by the thoughts of an Infinite Mind and that man, as a product of that creation, also possesses creative power through his controllable thought processes. Ponder this word from Sir James Jeans:

Today there is a wide measure of agreement, which on the physical side of science approaches almost to unanimity, that the stream of knowledge is heading toward a non-mechanical reality; the universe begins to look more like a great thought than like a great machine. Mind no longer appears as an accidental intruder into the realm of matter; we are beginning to suspect that we ought rather to hail it as the creator and governor of the realm of matter—not of course our individual minds, but the minds in which the atoms out of which our individual minds have grown exist as thoughts.

The new knowledge compels us to revise our hasty first impressions that we had stumbled into a universe which either did not concern itself with life or was actively hostile to life. The old dualism of mind and matter, which was mainly responsible for the supposed hostility, seems likely to disappear, not through matter becoming in any way more shadowy or insubstantial than heretofore, or through mind becoming resolved into a function of the working of matter, *but through substantial matter resolving itself into a creation and manifestation of mind*. We discover that the universe shows evidence of a designing or controlling power that has something in common with our own individual minds. . . .[1]

Approximately one-tenth of the human mind is conscious. This part of the mind can form reasoned judgments, can detect truth from falsehood through the use of critical powers. Whatever it chooses to accept and dwell upon gradually sinks into the nine-tenths of the mind that is unconscious where the character of these thoughts makes us or breaks us depending upon whether they are positive or negative, true or false.

The unconscious mind is uncritical. It accepts what the conscious mind dwells upon without question and proceeds to bring *that* into manifestation. In a previous volume (*Something to Stand On*, Chapter II) we related the remarkable experience of a student by the name of Don Houts. While under hypnosis, the hypnotist addressed Don's unconscious mind thus: "I am taking the letter 'E' out of your life completely until 9 A.M. tomorrow. After you awake you will not recognize the letter 'E' as being a part of the alphabet. You will not be able to spell a word correctly that has that letter in it. But promptly at 9 A.M. tomorrow your 'E' will be back in its accustomed place."

We saw in that chapter how Don's uncritical, unconscious mind accepted that suggestion and brought it into manifestation and how promptly at 9 A.M. the next day, Don's "E" was back in place again. It had to do it. It is the law of mind. A man under hypnosis is merely a man asleep. His conscious mind is simply not functioning. But his unconscious which never sleeps remains uncritically receptive to any suggestion made to it and proceeds to bring *that* into manifestation.

1 *The Mysterious Universe* by Sir James Jeans, pp. 186–187. Cambridge University Press. Used by permission.

Dr. Leslie G. Weatherhead once desired to demonstrate to a young lady the power of an idea accepted by the unconscious. Having put her under hypnosis, he told her he was going to touch her bare arm with a red-hot iron as he pressed the end of his fountain pen against her flesh. She screamed with pain. When he removed the pen there was a scar there exactly the same as though he had burned her with a poker. The power of the thought of the red-hot iron had been uncritically accepted by her unconscious and she will carry the scar of a third-degree burn to her grave!

Do you see the importance of all this? In this case a false thought accepted as true by the uncritical unconscious had the power to change enough bodily tissue *in one second* to leave a scar for life! That shows the creative power of thought!

Most of us will never be put under hypnosis. But we must remember that the same laws of mind are at work when we are normal and wide-awake. What our critical, conscious minds take as the truth is accepted by the unconscious and must be brought into manifestation. It is the law. It is the basis of all of Jesus' acts of healing. Again and again he said, "You must believe," or "According to your faith be it unto you." When his disciples failed to heal the epileptic boy and asked Jesus why they were powerless he said, "Because of your unbelief: for verily I say unto you, If ye have faith as a grain of mustard seed, ye shall say unto this mountain, Remove hence to your place; and it shall remove; and nothing shall be impossible to you." (Matt. 17:20)

When faith in the power of an indwelling God is added to belief in his healing power to affect an ailing body, we are giving our deep minds the raw material out of which so-called miracles are made. Only, instead of calling them miracles I think we should conceive of them as falling within the framework of spiritual law, albeit higher reaches of that law than man can as yet comprehend.

One of the most striking examples of the power of faith and positive thinking and affirmation to heal body, mind and affairs is to be found in Dr. Elwood Worcester's excellent book, *Body, Mind and Spirit*. It is so very good that I beg leave to quote the story in full:

Says Dr. Worcester:

Last spring I was present at a small gathering of men and women interested in medical psychology, to listen to an address by a famous man of science. After he had finished his formal talk, he said in effect: "Ladies and gentlemen, before I sit down I wish to make a more personal statement which I think you will find of greater interest and value than my lecture. Up to my fiftieth year [he is now about sixty-five] I was an unhappy, ineffective man. None of the works on which my reputation rests was published. I was making my home in an unimportant town in California and was utterly unknown in the scientific world. I lived in a constant sense of gloom and failure. Perhaps my most painful symptom was a blinding headache which recurred usually two days of the week, during which I could do nothing.

"As my fiftieth birthday approached, I began to take stock of my soul and I realized that something was very wrong with me. I had read some of the literature of New Thought, which at the time appeared to be buncombe, and some statement of William James on the directing of attention to what is good and useful and ignoring the rest. One saying of his stuck in my mind, 'We might have to give up our philosophy of evil, but what is that in comparison with gaining a life of goodness?' (or words to that effect). Hitherto these doctrines had seemed to me only mystical theories, but realizing that my soul was sick and growing worse and that my life was intolerable, I determined to put them to the proof. In accordance with my teaching and mental habits, I resolved to make a careful, honest experiment which should be as carefully and honestly recorded. I decided to limit the period of conscious effort to one month, as I thought this time long enough to prove its value or its worthlessness to me. During this month I resolved to impose certain restrictions on my thoughts. If I thought of the past, I would try to let my mind dwell only on its happy, pleasing incidents, the bright days of my childhood, the inspiration of my teachers and the slow revelation of my life-work. In thinking of the present, I would deliberately turn my attention to its desirable elements, my home, the opportunities my solitude gave me to work, and so on, and I resolved to make the utmost use of these opportunities and to ignore the fact that they seemed to lead to nothing. In thinking of the future I determined to regard every worthy and possible ambition as within my grasp. Ridiculous as this seemed at the time, in view of what has come to me since, I see that the only defect of my plan was that it aimed too low and did not include enough.

"By this time I felt that I was about to make an important discovery and I began to be conscious of a certain tingling expectation which I usually experience in my scientific work at such moments. When the day I had assigned arrived, I threw myself into the new task (incomparably the greatest I had ever attempted to perform) with ardour. I did not have to wait a month. At the end of eight days, I knew the experiment was succeeding. I had not thought of including my headaches in my scheme of effort, as I deemed these beyond the possibility of help from this source. But therein I miscalculated, as they abruptly ceased. In fifteen years I have had but one headache and that was one I deliberately brought on for experimental purposes.

"Apart from this welcome relief, the first change of which I was aware was that whereas for many years I had been profoundly unhappy, I now felt happy and contented. I knew what James meant when he spoke of 'being consciously right and superior.' What surprised me more was that I was able to make others happy and that my personality seemed to attract, whereas before it had repelled. Up to this point of my recital I anticipate that you will find nothing strange in these changes and discoveries, except that I made them so late in life. What follows may tax your credulity. Personally I should not have accepted one of these statements sixteen years ago. Yet most of the changes in my outer life are matters of fact which can be verified in *Who's Who*. As I stated at the beginning, the burdens I found hardest to bear were bringing me no nearer the goal of my ambition, that although my capacity was considerable, my name was unknown and my works unpublished because no publisher would accept them.

"The outward changes of my life resulting from my change of thought have surprised me more than the inward changes, yet they spring from the latter. There were certain eminent men, for example, whose recognition I deeply craved. The foremost of those wrote me, out of a clear sky, and invited me to become his assistant. My works have all been published, and a foundation has been created to publish all that I may write in the future. The men with whom I have worked have been helpful and cooperative toward me chiefly on account of my changed disposition. Formerly they would not have endured me. One ambition of mine, my election to the presidency of a great foreign scientific society, though in accordance with my highest hope, seemed so utterly beyond my reach that I should have deemed it preposterous to aim at it, yet it came to me. As I look back over all these changes, it seems to me that in some blind way I stumbled on a *path of life* and set forces to working for me which before were against me.

"There is one more incident I must record. After several years of peace and improvement it occurred to me that I had not given these theories sufficient test. Apparently my experiment had succeeded, and I knew too much about the law of probability to ascribe all these changes to chance. Still, as a scientific man, I felt that I ought to test the principles with which I had been working negatively. I, therefore, began deliberately to revive the emotions of fear and apprehension. Within two hours I felt myself weak, depressed, doubtful, and I was conscious, for the last time, of a splitting headache. I, therefore, felt that I had done my duty and that I might rest comfortably in the great saying of Paul: 'All things work together for good to them that love God.' "

Dr. Worcester concludes:

If it were right for me to mention a great name, that of one of the least credulous or superstitious of mankind, this recital of his would evoke no mockery.[2]

God is no respecter of persons. He plays no favorites. What he did for this famous scientist he can do for you and me *if we will pay the price.* And I am now going to challenge every reader of these words to make this experiment: Go on a seven-day mental diet. Start every day with prayer and meditation. Ask God to forgive the weaknesses and sins of the past. Accept that forgiveness so as to start with a clean slate. Commune with God often through each day. Live on a spiritual mountain-top. Think of *all* men as interesting and infinitely worthful sons of God. Allow no negative thought to find lodgment in the mind. Think of every task and every personal contact as a thrilling opportunity for an interesting experience and a chance for service.

It has been truly said that the difference between a successful and an unsuccessful marriage may lie in leaving three or four things a day unsaid. That may also be just the difference between harmonious or discordant human relations outside the family, married or unmarried. Such self-control will only be possible if the mind is deliberately fixed continuously on the love, radiance and poise of the Indwelling Presence.

This will depend upon an inner control that *can* be ours but that, in turn, will result only from a deliberately planned strategy. If the suggestion that "life is too hard" comes to mind, be ready with "I can do all things through Christ which strengtheneth me." In the place of "I have had one blow after another," cry with Paul, "I have fought a good fight, I have kept the faith." Instead of "I'm afraid," hear God say to Joshua and to *you*, "Have not I commanded thee? *Be strong and of a good courage; be not afraid, neither be thou dismayed; for the Lord thy God is with thee whithersoever thou goest.*"

To be really *alive* for seven days! Are you with me? Is your desire for harmony in *all* of life's relationships, for better physical, mental

2 Reprinted from *Body, Mind and Spirit* by Elwood Worcester and Samuel McComb; copyright 1931 by Charles Scribner's Sons; used by permission of the publishers.

and spiritual health strong enough and deep enough to keep you on the job for seven days? Can you start and end *every* day with a fifteen-minute time in communion with the Eternal Presence and then tune in many other times a day as you work and play?

If so—give me your hand! This day and this hour represent the turning point in your life and heaven's richest rewards are already yours! "What is that?" you say. *"Already* yours?" Yes, already yours. Listen to Jesus' positive assurance on that: "That is why I tell you, as to whatever you pray and make request for, *if you believe that you have received it, it shall be yours."* (Mark 11:24—Weymouth translation)[3] That is real faith. It is an atmosphere of *quiet confidence* in the power of God to create the new condition and "in quietness and confidence shall be your strength."

Give yourself and God a break—seven days of mountain-top living —with never a single slip. When tempted to go negative for even a moment make this great affirmation: *"God is radiant Light, Shining Beauty, Contagious Joy, Creative Power, All Pervading Love, Purity, Serenity. And these attributes of the character of God are flowing through me now like a crystal stream."*

Power to you, my friend!

 ## LEARN TO LET GO

The other evening after I had retired for the night, I switched on the light at the head of my bed and picked up Thoreau's *Walden.* I followed this remarkable man's revolt against the speed of the civilization of his day. Ninety-six years ago he was fuming against the mad people who wanted to travel "thirty miles an hour." "I went to the woods because I wished to live deliberately," he writes, "to front only the essential facts of life, and see if I could not learn what it had to teach and not, when I came to die, discover that I had not lived."

One wonders what our Concord sage would have written today about the speed-crazed people who drive eighty or ninety miles an hour on busy highways; what he would have thought of the radio and television and planes that travel faster than sound—going pre-

3 *Weymouth's New Testament in Modern Speech.* Published by Harper & Brothers. Used by permission.

cisely nowhere. Walden ought to be required reading once a year for every person over fifteen years of age in the whole United States.

The other day I passed an island in Basswood Lake on the Canadian border whereon a man had built a cabin to "get away from this speed crazed age." But the poor man already had a "for sale" sign up because the tide of restless humanity was already pouring around his wilderness hideout, and I was told he was looking for another island far up in the wilds of Canada. He had my sympathy!

In an article in the *Nation* (June 18, 1949) entitled "Ulcers and History" we were shocked to learn how many men in public life develop ulcers—the disease caused by worry and frustration. Here were some of them: James V. Forrestal; General Marshall; Senator Austin, Chief U.S. delegate to the United Nations; General Bedell Smith, former Ambassador to Moscow; General Clay; General Eisenhower; Secretaries Hull, Stettinius and Byrnes; and Under Secretary Sumner Wells; plus nearly all of the President's Cabinet. The two key figures in Britain—Sir Stafford Cripps and Ernest Bevin had ulcers. The sad truth is that the decisions that may affect the future destinies of every living human being on earth were then being made by sick men! And these men were made sick by fear, tension, worry and anxiety!

Certain it is that the speed and tension of modern life is rapidly sapping our reserves of strength and sanity. Our greatest problem is how to deal with our nervous tensions; how calmly "to front the essential facts of life" so as to learn how to live serenely and purposefully; in short, how to let go of worry, tension and fear.

First of all, we need to grasp the basic fact that nervous tension is of the mind. The sickness is there and the cure is there too. Stationed at the threshold of consciousness is the eternal "I am." It has the power of life and death, of happiness or despair over the central self through its power to accept or reject trains of thought. It is the feeder of the unconscious mind. If it learns how to hang on to those thoughts that are full of faith, hope and love, the unconscious mind will take them in and use them for building a personality marked by poise, peace and power. That is, it will, provided—provided it also learns to let go of all negative, fear-inspired, tension-building thoughts. So we must learn to "let go" in this streamlined age of high tension.

Let go of tense muscles. Dr. David Harold Fink, in his interesting book, *Release from Nervous Tension,* has several chapters on release from physical nervous strain. He tells us to get into a comfortable reclining position and then talk to the muscles. Start with the face. Tell the eyes to "Let go. Let go." Tell the muscles of the cheeks and of the mouth to "Let go." Visualize the command being carried out. Picture the entire face in utter repose.

Then go on to the arms and hands. Command them to relax; then on down to the chest and lungs; tell the lungs to breathe deeply, slowly and rhythmically—and keep the mind there for some time to see that this command is really carried out. Let the mind then wander leisurely to the legs and feet: "Let go! Let go! Let go still more!" Dr. Fink warns us that it will take at least ten or twelve weeks of this before we begin to approximate maximum results. To be sure, we will notice remarkable benefits at once—the very first time we try it for half an hour. But we have been tense so long that a long-time correctional program is imperative.

This is only a beginning. We have not yet even touched the primary cause of these tight muscles. That cause lies buried deep in the mind and spirit. As David Grayson wrote, after spending six months in bed: "Nowhere with more freedom from trouble does a man retire than into his own soul." For "tranquillity is nothing else than the good ordering of the mind." Such "good ordering" involves letting go of a lot of things.

We must let go of fancied slights. Most people do not mean to hurt us. The average slight is the result of preoccupation or accident. When the colossal statue of the Christ of the Andes was erected on the border between Argentina and Chile years ago, it was made from the melted bullets that symbolized the end of a long and bloody strife. When certain Chileans noticed, however, that this towering Christ was facing Argentina, the word soon flew from lip to lip that this was an intentional insult to Chile. Christ had turned his back on them! War almost resulted before a Santiago newspaper editorial pointed out that this was the greatest compliment that Christ could possibly pay to Chile: by turning his back on Chile and gazing out toward Argentina, Christ showed by his very posture who needed watching! Soon everybody in both countries was laughing heartily over a most timely and clever editorial and the threat of war was gone. A little humor and a better perspective helps us to "let go" of suspicion and hatred.

A barefoot boy of four was walking along a shady village street one hot August afternoon eating an ice-cream cone. Suddenly a group of older boys came dashing around a corner, knocked the little fellow down in their rush, and dashed his cone to the ground. The lad sat up and stared at the incomprehensible tragedy before him. There were no words, no tears; just mute, wide-eyed agony.

An old lady had seen it all from her front porch. Summoning all of the wisdom garnered in three score years and ten she approached the boy: "Well, laddie," she said, "the very worst has happened to you. But stand up and I'll show you something." The little fellow got to his feet. "Now, put your right foot on top of your ice cream, step hard, and watch the cool, yellow, beautiful stuff come right up through your toes!"

The boy did as directed and the ice cream shot up through his toes. The old lady laughed with glee. "I'll bet there isn't another boy in this whole town who has ever tickled his toes on a hot day with ice cream," she chuckled. "Now run home and tell your mother about your funny experience. And always remember," she added, "whatever happens you can still have fun."

I can almost hear somebody saying: "I, too, could 'let go' of an ice cream cone, barefooted or not; it only cost him a nickel. But take my case now . . ." Maybe so. But before you go on to state it, take a walk with Addison through Westminster Abbey and have a good look around. Then follow him back to his office and peer over his shoulder as he writes a piece for the *Spectator*, Number 26: "When I see kings lying by those who deposed them," (I, myself, found it necessary to take time out here for a good look out the window to ponder this at length) "when I consider holy men that divided the world with their contests and disputes placed side by side, I reflect with sorrow and astonishment on the little competitions, factions, and debates of mankind. When I read the several dates on the tombs, of some that died yesterday and some six hundred years ago, I consider that great day when we shall all of us be contemporaries and make our appearance together." How does that make your pet grievance look?

We must let go of hatred! Regardless of what the object of our hatred has done, we must realize that this poisoned passion will hurt us far more than it will our enemy. When Leonardo da Vinci was beginning work on his immortal "Last Supper," he had a violent quarrel with a fellow painter. So bitter and enraged did Leonardo become that he conceived and carried into execution the plan to paint the face of his enemy into the face of Judas. As he painted he doted upon the thought that his revenge was the more sweet since the influence of the act would be remembered for generations.

The face of Judas was one of the first that he finished and everyone could easily recognize the face of his artist enemy. All went well until he came to paint the face of Christ and then he could make no progress. Something seemed to be holding him in check and frustrating his best efforts. Then it came to him—the hatred in his heart that had been painted into the face of Judas—that was impeding his work. So he painted out the face of Judas and commenced anew on the face of Jesus with the magnificent result which the ages have acclaimed.

We must let go of worry! I have never yet seen worriers who would deny that worrying was futile business because it has never helped to solve a problem. On the contrary, they readily admit that worrying impedes any possible solution.

I recently read of a man who went to a doctor for a physical checkup and was told to "slow down and stop worrying or you're through." The man thereupon went to Florida to hunt ducks and stop stewing about business. On two successive days he got the legal limit—ten ducks. On the third day he had eight by four in the afternoon but he missed a few and then began to fret and worry lest he miss some more and go back to the hotel "to face the other guests with only eight ducks!" In this mood he couldn't hit the side of a barn.

Suddenly a violent reaction set in. "Why, you fool," he said to himself. "Here you are throwing a fit because you don't possess two measly ducks when you already have eight. What are you, a game-hog?" He had a good laugh at himself and sat there perfectly relaxed and content. At that moment, two ring-necks swung over his decoys at sixty miles an hour and he got them both. He was still relaxed!

That night he relived the incident and then made what he called a "staggering discovery." In life, too, he already had eight ducks! At forty-nine he was close to the lawful limit of his heart's desire. But he had not been happy. He was worrying so much about the two ducks he didn't need that he had no appreciation of the eight he had. He counted up his eight ducks—a sweet wife, children of whom he was proud, friends, a good living, a fair share of honors, wide interests, a hopeful outlook. The only two ducks he didn't have were as much money or as much fame as some men had. Well—was he going to stew himself into his grave over that? Certainly not! No, sir! Whenever he found himself beginning to push the blood pressure up he would stop and count his eight ducks—and relax.

Note the mental dexterity, poise and sense of humor displayed by the little fellow who called his Dad into the back yard to see him knock a fly over the back fence to prove what a great batter he was. Tossing the ball up in the air, he took a mighty swing at it—and missed. "Strike one!" he yelled, transforming himself on the instant from a batter into an eagle-eyed umpire. A second time he tossed the ball, a second time the mighty swing and a miss. "Strike two!" he yelled with a grin. "Only takes one to sock it, Pop," he said. "Watch this one." Once more the tossed ball, the mighty cut and the sad thud as the horsehide hit the ground. "Yer out!" yelled the umpire. Was the batter crestfallen? Not this one. Turning a beaming face to his father as they headed in for supper he said, "Boy, Dad, am I ever a pitcher!" That lad knew how and when to let go!

All that we have said is true but we have not yet dealt with the very heart of our problem. A man does not let go of his worry and fear and tenseness just by telling himself the time has come to do so. Because, you see, these things are primarily caused by a feeling of insecurity which in turn results from a lack of faith in God. Chalmers' great phrase, "the expulsive power of a new affection," comes alive just here. When we bring our insecurity, our sin, our worry to Christ; when we take a real look at him as the one quiet, beautifully poised, self-assured person in the courtroom of Pontius Pilate; when we suddenly realize that he "let go" of everything including life itself—except his crystal-clear consciousness of God, we are ready also to let go—to lose our souls to find them again. God becomes real. We develop a feeling of security, even as Jesus did, and our new affection magically exercises its expulsive power as we let go of a lot of useless baggage.

So, if we would learn to "let go" of our taut muscles and nerves, of our anxiety for the future, we must find a new security in the only place where the real thing ultimately resides—in God. As Dr. A. E. Day says: "Instead of complaints, protests, pleas, arguments, entreaties, what he wants from us is a chance to talk, to inform, to correct, to illumine, to comfort, to alter, to 'clean house,' to strengthen, to ennoble. That requires from us passivity, 'alert passivity,' it is true, but still the very opposite of the clamorous, insistent, 'keyed-up' self we usually bring to the hour of prayer." Such communion will convince us that eight ducks are enough!

WHEN SOMEONE BELIEVES IN YOU

When I was eighteen years of age, just out of high school, I determined to work my way through college selling books. The Volume Library appealed to me as the best single-volume reference work in the world. It still does. I was timid and inexperienced but I was willing to tackle Bay City, Michigan, and show the world that even a timid boy could sell such a remarkable book.

During the first four days I took not a single order. Everywhere I went they instantly pulled a Standard Dictionary of Facts off the shelf and said they had bought it the summer before and that it was filling their needs. I sat down that fourth evening and wrote the company a doleful report and asked for some new territory.

Never shall I forget the contents of the special delivery letter that came back by return mail. Mr. R. E. Trosper wrote as follows:

I am surprised beyond words to learn that L. L. Dunnington thinks he can't sell Volume Libraries in Bay City! I knew all about the number of Standard Dictionary of Facts sold there last year. That is why I sent *you* to Bay City. I knew you believed enough in the superior character of the Volume Library to sell it right over the Standard Dictionary without ever batting an eye. Most of our men couldn't—but you *can*. I still believe you can do it. Now get out into the field tomorrow and go to it. I believe you have the ability to stay there all summer and fill that town full of our superior product.

I read that letter a dozen times before going to bed. I prayed about the matter, as was my custom, and some time in the night made up my mind that I would never let Mr. Trosper down. If he had faith in me

I would show him his confidence was not misplaced. The next day I was terrific! I made ten canvasses; sold ten Volume Libraries; collected a dollar down on seven of the sales; and sent Trosper a report that he relayed to every salesman in the organization. And I did stay in Bay City all summer!

There is so little difference between success and failure—often just the difference of being fortunate enough to have some discerning soul express the fact that he believes in you in spite of everything. Many a man has failed simply because some thoughtless or cantankerous soul gave him a kick instead of a boost.

The late William Henry Eustice was one of the best mayors Minneapolis ever had. He was fearless and honest and generous. His large fortune was wisely spent for the good of needy humanity. At the age of twelve he had been stricken with infantile paralysis and lay a helpless cripple for four years. By indomitable will, however, and superhuman effort, the little fellow managed to educate himself while in bed so that, at the age of seventeen, he was able to hobble across country on crutches and secure a position teaching school. At nineteen he proudly applied for entrance in a small college and was admitted on trial. One week later an instructor with a limited social vision told him he was incapable of carrying college work and advised him to leave school at once. At the moment that Eustice needed a word of praise, he was slapped down.

Throughout the night the lad fought the issue through. His discouragement mounted until, shortly after midnight, he determined to take his life. By a strange whim of fate it was the rope that broke instead of his neck. By morning the dark mood of despair had passed and he determined to prove to all doubters that he could graduate from college. Ultimately he did not only that but he made a record of public usefulness and service that was outstanding.

During the dark night of his blackest hours Eustice would have had a lot of sympathy for a certain prosperous farmer's wife in Ohio. She wrote to a friend:

Maybe when I'm deaf and blind and a hundred years old I'll get used to having everything I do taken for granted. As it is, life comes pretty dull and hard when you don't hear a word of thanks for all your efforts to keep things nice and bright. It isn't easy to keep on doing your best when you're never told whether your cooking is good or not. Sometimes I feel like copying the woman who served her menfolk cattle fodder one day for dinner, after waiting twenty years for a word of praise. "I've never heard aught to make me think you'd know the difference," she said when they declared she must be crazy.

"The plumb-line of democracy by which its walls are built straight and true is the American social faith in the intrinsic and potential worth of every human person," says John W. Studebaker, U.S. Commissioner of Education. That social faith stems straight from Jesus of Nazareth. It is Christian to the core. Every follower of Christ readily admits that he believes it but he does not always act as though he did. A word of just praise or an expression of faith in us at judicious intervals acts like a tonic to our flagging energies. Even a farmer's wife cannot be expected to go on forever preparing tasty meals without some indication from the rest of the family that her contribution to their well-being is appreciated. When it comes from sincere hearts something from the very deeps of her being responds and the work becomes light again.

How the plainest of us respond to a call of danger when we feel we are needed and somebody indicates he believes we are up to the hazards involved. Do you remember that stirring scene from Mrs. Miniver? The British had been defeated at Dunkirk. A broken and despairing army was pouring out of Belgium onto the beaches. A day or two and the German air force would finish the boys off like dead ducks.

Then came the call. Telephones in England rang all night long in the dark and every man who had any kind of a boat at all was groping about his bedroom and pulling on his clothes. One by one they were all wanted somewhere. The English Admiralty was calling all skippers, big and little, and the Admiralty had faith that England's sons would respond.

They did. Launches, tugs, yachts and outboard motors—everything that could float and move—came chugging bravely out of coves and inlets and headed for Dunkirk. Nameless folks, moving bravely through the fog in the very presence of death and turning the tide of history—together! Somebody had enough faith in them to call them, so they did what the Germans thought was the impossible.

As I left Davenport for Iowa City in a driving rain one day, I picked up a fine-looking lad in uniform. It was Dick Wise, aged nineteen, of Boys Town, Nebraska. When I mentioned having seen the movie by that name Dick's face beamed. "That's just what it is like," he said. "And Father Flanagan! What a man! He took me in when I was eight. I don't know to this day who my parents were or where I was born. All I know is that Father Flanagan took me in, believed in me, and was a father to me. I'll never let him down—never."

Nor has he. Here is Dick's amazing story. He ran away and joined the army at fourteen, lying about his age. He became a paratrooper and jumped behind the Japanese lines. He was shot in the leg before reaching the ground. Two buddies who rushed out with a stretcher to get him were both killed. A bit later the Japanese carried him to a hospital. Both ankles were broken. For eighteen months he was a prisoner. He was forced to work in a factory while still on crutches and, when he could not work fast enough, he was beaten so severely that they broke his back. "But I can honestly say I didn't hate them," said Dick. "Father Flanagan taught us never to hate even our enemies and I couldn't let him down."

When the barracks was bombed and burned, Dick gave his two blankets to his guard's wife because hers were burned. This so surprised the guards that they thereafter secretly showed him many courtesies that made his existence more tolerable.

"And was I ever lucky," said Dick. Up came his left hand to show me he had no knuckles. "On one job," he said, "a certain foreman thought I was loafing so he hit me across the knuckles with a hatchet and broke every one of them. When the Americans released us, I was flown to the U.S.A. on the *Dead Duck*. In a Denver hospital, they made me run the scale on a piano with the fingers of that hand and I finally learned to play. There must have been some musical talent in my family somewhere because, though I can't read a note, I can play anything by ear that I have ever heard." When he said he had given a concert in the Denver Civic Auditorium and mentioned several classical numbers he had rendered I was skeptical. But when I brought Dick home to lunch and he made a bee line for our piano I was convinced. He had said that Percy Grainger had heard him play and had offered him a scholarship at his Summer Camp in Interlochen, Michigan. I don't doubt it. And all of that from a boy of nineteen from Boys Town because Father Flanagan believed in him!

How Jesus believed in men! No matter what they had done, no matter how low they had fallen, he saw unlimited possibilities in them. As though to answer the cynic who might say that Jesus was fooled by always looking at men through rose-colored glasses John wrote: "He did not need to have anyone tell him what was in man, for he *knew* what was in man." He knew how Mary Magdalene made a living; but he succeeded in convincing her that God loved her; that he himself believed in her and that vast possibilities in character development lay all unclaimed in the deeps of her being. How many young people there are in America right now, living on the plane of a Mary Magdalene, who would turn abruptly from their unhappy, low-level existence, if the right and convincing word were uttered to prove to them that God still loves them and believes in them; that his forgiveness is ever ready to be given; that all of the resources of the Heavenly Powers may be theirs to speed them into a new life!

One of the most remarkable public schools in the country is New York's P.S. 37. A visitor, greeted with a warm, friendly "good morning" by the boys as they passed down the hall, would never suspect that those boys had formerly been among the city's incorrigibles. All two hundred and fifty of them, however, are there because other schools could not handle them. At least half have had court experience and many were sent to P.S. 37 as a last resort before commitment to correctional institutions.

Out of this raw material Mrs. Rashkis, the principal, and her teachers have developed a school whose standards of interest, courtesy and good behavior are considerably above average. According to the testimony of Judge Juvenal Marchisio of the New York Domestic Relations Court, the school salvages more than ninety per cent of its pupils for future citizenship.

Read the full account of this remarkable school in an article by Elsie McCormick in *Survey Graphic* (April 1945). When a boy is transferred to P.S. 37, he is usually brought by a truant officer. He is surly and defiant. He expects tough treatment. He is not at all prepared to have other "tough guys" shush him down with the remark that his toughness is just "kid stuff." The attention he has always had from such conduct is no longer forthcoming.

Here, for example, was Solly, a boy from a comfortable middle-class home. At his previous school he had refused to say a word in class; a sneer was always on his face. After two weeks at P.S. 37 Mrs. Rashkis made him her office boy. He became so interested in running errands that he forgot his sneer.

Then he told Mrs. Rashkis his story. His brilliant brother, destined for a professional career, got all his mother's concern and affection. "I just thought there was no use of my even trying," said Solly. Mrs. Rashkis soon convinced him that he had great possibilities wrapped up in his growing life and that she believed in him. Today he is a congenial, useful member of society.

Another boy, well known to the truant officers, was given a job running the motion picture machine. He went through two terms without being late or absent once. "I never was in a school before where they really needed me," he said.

"The tendency of teachers and parents is not to trust a problem boy with a responsible job," says Mrs. Rashkis, "yet such a job often proves to be effective moral medicine." George could not adjust himself to his stepfather and his unhappiness expressed itself in temper tantrums and truancy. Six schools had dismissed him before he arrived at P.S. 37. He showed his first sign of interest when the principal asked the boys to suggest a good way of storing and distributing the midmorning milk. George's plan was accepted and George was put in charge. It solved his problem and he and his stepfather became good pals.

Here is an arresting statement in reference to these boys: "In nine times out of ten, the blame rests on the parents. Of 65 boys recently studied, only four had homes that were satisfactory. Again and again the reports show squalor, indifference, lack of understanding, cruel treatment, perpetual family rows, divorce, and parents who are seldom at home."

There is no substitute in all this world for a home where there is love and understanding; for parents who conceive it to be their chief function in life to furnish an environment for their children that reflects selflessness, honesty and poise and that eventuates in good character. When will our parents awaken to a realization of the character-forming magic that is wrapped up in the sincere affirmation: *"I believe in you, I trust you, because I love you"?* America will have better children when she has better parents. And we shall have better parents when more of them find the radiance and peace of Christ in their own hearts.

BETTER TO LIGHT A CANDLE

"Better to light one candle than to curse the darkness"— so goes an old Chinese proverb. It is so easy to curse the darkness of injustice and evil without doing the least thing to dispel that darkness. Jesus said, "Ye are the light of the world. A city that is set on a hill cannot be hid. Neither do men light a candle, and put it under a bushel, but on a candlestick; and it giveth light unto all that are in the house. Let your light so shine that men may see your good works. . . ."

Church membership in the United States now totals over 80 million people or 53 per cent of the nation's population as over against 22 per cent in 1890. Every one of these members should be lighted candles dispelling darkness, but all too many of them feel that they are helpless little persons without influence. This is simply not true. Even the humblest of us with the will to do so may wield a tremendous influence for the building of a better world.

In a small California town a young Negro had a part-time job in a filling station so he could support himself and wife as he studied to become a teacher. Certain prejudiced white people objected to buying gasoline from a colored boy, however, and the owner was about to fire the boy when a certain woman appeared and asked how many customers he thought he would lose if he continued to keep the boy on the payroll. After a moment's thought the owner thought he might lose as many as twenty. "Will you keep him on if I get you twenty new customers?" asked our friend. "You bet I will," said the surprised proprietor. Not only did she do as promised but she brought in five more for good measure!

This woman was a Christopher, one of a growing band of men and women united in the purpose to help change our world into a better place. Although under Catholic auspices, the movement embraces all faiths. There are no chapters, no committees, no meetings, no dues. From a central office in New York occasional bulletins are mailed out to over one hundred thousand interested persons. Each of these people merely believes it is better to light one candle than to curse the darkness; that he can, alone and unaided, strike a series of telling blows in the war of good against evil and that he can, therefore, actually change the world.

An unknown Italian barber from Southampton, Long Island, was one of the most powerful influences in turning the Communist tide in Italy two or three years ago at a moment when a Communist victory at the polls would undoubtedly have changed the course of affairs in all of Europe. Grateful beyond words for the freedom and opportunity he enjoyed in his adopted country and fearful of the slavery that faced his relatives in Italy should Communism triumph, he wrote his relatives glowing accounts of how happy men could be under this kind of government. He persuaded his friends to do likewise. He appealed to newspaper editors and even to President Truman to help enlist the nation. Veterans groups, civic organizations, G.I. brides from overseas caught the spirit of the campaign until the trickle of letters swelled to a mighty torrent. This undoubtedly helped to turn the tide at the polls toward a victory that heartened the world. The power of this particular lighted candle is proof enough that men who love freedom need never lose that freedom if they will positively exert themselves instead of cursing the darkness.

We should thank God that He has made us in such a way that opposition to a cause that is dear to our hearts merely strengthens the resolve of normal men to fight on through to victory. Arnold J. Toynbee illustrated the value of opposition in an article in the *Woman's Home Companion* (August 1949 issue). Fishermen off the coast of England have a real problem in keeping herring fresh and lively until they can be marketed. These sensitive fish are trapped and dumped into huge tanks on a trawler's deck. But herring seem to know when they are prisoners. They tend to stop swimming, turn sluggish and lose color and freshness.

One captain discovered a trick however which kept his catch fresh and lively right to the dock. *He put one catfish into each tank!* This natural enemy of the herring kept the fish in rapid movement. To be sure he ate a few but that was no more than his just reward. The rest brought a better price on the market.

Mr. Toynbee suggests that in the herring tank which we call the western world, Russian Communism is the obliging catfish and Providence the resourceful captain. Lunacharsky, first Commissar for Education under the Soviets once wrote in *Izvestia:* "We hate Christianity and Christians. Even the best of them must be considered our worst enemies. They preach love of one's neighbor and mercy which is contrary to our principles. What we want is hate. . . . Only then will we conquer the Universe."

There is a challenge for us! Such a catfish will eat every herring in the tank if these little fish ever stop swimming. The United States government is spending billions of dollars that it has to borrow from our people in order to help poverty-stricken Europeans raise their standard of living and thus withstand the false promises of the Communists. This is love and mercy and justice in action and we shall one day see whether love and mercy or hatred is the stronger power.

I am reminded at this point of a remarkable letter which a thirteen-year-old Japanese girl wrote not long ago "to some schoolgirl in Australia." As you read keep in mind that Australian law bars from its territory all persons of the so-called yellow race. In spite of that fact, school authorities in both countries have encouraged the exchange of letters between "pen friends." One of these letters published by "World's Children" was written by a girl from the Shinagawa Girls' High School. She neglected to say that she lost her right hand from an incendiary bomb that was dropped by a member of the white race. Here is the letter:

I am afraid you may not like receiving this letter or answering it because I am Japanese. But I hope it is not so. I am not your enemy. It may help a little if I tell you that I too have suffered—my three brothers, they are all asleep; my house, it is burnt. Out of all this cruelty and hatred and mistake, could we not arrange that there be peace and prosperity and happiness for all countries? I want it that way. Even to a war-scarred land like mine, spring will come. It is coming now, with plum-blossom and cherry and happiness and warmth. How do we arrange that it might be spring for all the world? I would beg you to believe that I write this letter not with my pen, but with my heart.

HIDOKE INOURIE

This is a little girl who is lighting a candle in the midst of the darkness of the white man's Exclusion Act. Who can say how far its tiny light may spread? Three brothers killed by white men—house burnt—right hand gone—country defeated and destitute. Yet "out of all this cruelty and hatred and mistake, could *we* not arrange that there be peace and prosperity and happiness for all countries? I want it that way!" Can any darkness ultimately destroy such a brilliant little light as that?

The freedom of the press, of speech and of assembly which we enjoy so much in this country, but which we take for granted, was not always ours. We came by it the hard way. Certain intrepid and fearless souls took their very lives in their hands and battled the most terrific opposition before they won it.

Come back with me for a moment to a summer day on August 4, 1735, in the small town of New York. The royal governor of the colony of New York was a corrupt official by the name of William Crosby. He was notorious for his cruelty and greed. He had the habit of thrusting his hand into the treasury for his private gain and of sending citizens to jail if they objected.

There was only one newspaper in the colony—*The New York Journal*—edited by one John Peter Zenger. The editor had dared to expose the governor in a series of hard-hitting articles and consequently on this fourth day of August, 1735, he found himself in jail. He was denied counsel nor was he even allowed to talk with anybody except his wife and then only through a hole in the door.

The prosecution declared to the jury that the *truth* of the charges against the governor was not for them to consider. All they needed to decide was whether the said Mr. Zenger actually printed the statements against the King's representative. "According to the laws of Charles I," shouted the prosecution, "any criticism of an officer of the government is libel, whether true or false."

At that moment there was a stir in the back of the courtroom as Andrew Hamilton slowly made his way down the center aisle. This most distinguished attorney in the colonies had heard of Zenger's plight and, in spite of the fact that he was an infirm old man, he had jogged his long, weary way from Philadelphia via stage coach at his own expense to strike a blow for freedom.

Looking squarely into the eyes of the rugged men of the jury, Mr. Hamilton declared that the statements which Mr. Zenger had printed were known to be the truth and to call truth a libel "is a sword in the

hands of a wicked King and an errant coward to destroy the innocent." "The question before you, gentlemen of the jury," Hamilton
cried, "is not of small nor private concern; it is not the cause of a
poor printer, nor of New York alone, which you are now trying. No!
It may in its consequence affect every free man in America. It is the
best cause. It is the cause of liberty. Every man who prefers freedom
to a life of slavery will bless and honor you as men who have baffled
the attempt of tyranny and, by an impartial verdict, have laid a noble
foundation for securing ourselves, our posterity and our neighbors
that to which nature and the laws have given us a right: the liberty
both of exposing and opposing arbitrary power by speaking and
writing Truth!"

The chief justice was furious. He instructed the jury to ignore the
plea of Mr. Hamilton and bring in a verdict of "Guilty." But it was
to no avail. In a few moments the jury filed back into the box and
pronounced the fateful words "Not Guilty" as the crowd broke into
prolonged applause. Thus the candle which was that day lighted by
an infirm old man sent its tiny rays down into the future to another
day when the freedom of the press was finally written into the Constitution of the new nation as Amendment I to the Bill of Rights.
Our nation has jealously guarded that sacred right through the years
and because of that fact it has recently been written into a universal
Bill of Rights for the United States.

The philosophy of the lighted candle has even deeper significance,
however, than the assurance that one person can change the world for
the better. For, when we give our whole selves in some good cause,
we automatically turn the stream of consciousness away from self
and out toward God and the world. And when we do that, we open the
way for God to build something of eternal value into our own lives
which eventuates in better health and wholeness of body, mind and
spirit.

Here is one example out of many that could be cited. An epileptic
girl, bed-bound in a California hospital, wrote an article for a small-
town newspaper in which she said that we should all "concentrate
on the good life around us instead of just the opposite." When readers
of that paper learned that this wise and courageous advice came from
a girl afflicted with epilepsy, a quantity of fan-mail poured in and
our brave little girl was soon writing a daily column—and soon on

the way to recovery! In lighting a candle for others she was lighting one for herself. In the spiritual economy of God's moral universe we profit personally in health and happiness in the proportion that we try to give these coveted prizes to the world of men. A candle lighted for others throws its beneficent rays in two directions—out and in.

We have cited some rather striking examples of the beneficent power of light as it has sent its healing beams abroad from certain personalities. The place where the candle most needs to burn with a steady and continuous flame is in our homes. Jesus said that such a candle "giveth light unto all that are *in the house*." It was his belief that all radiance of personality is borrowed radiance coming straight from the central Sun which is God; that daily communion with our heavenly Father is the one indispensable medium through which the soul's light may be kept continuously burning; that the darkness of fear, inferiority, insecurity and boredom may be banished from any home through the candle light of faith. Is your inner light glowing amid the confusions and despairs of our time?

LIFE'S GRACIOUS OVERFLOW

One hears a great deal these days about the necessity of dispensing justice. The small countries of the world must be given a just peace; the laboring man cares not for charity but he does demand justice from his employer; the criminal likewise must receive just punishment and remedial action.

With all of this and much more in the same temper, we are in complete accord. What doth the Lord require of thee but to do justly, to love mercy and to walk humbly with thy God? The Old Testament is full of demands for justice for all men.

But justice is not enough. The ideal of justice is quite inadequate for the needs of modern life. The chaos toward which our civilization is plunging with such reckless and frightening speed will never be transmitted into harmony through the application of justice alone. The added ingredient needed is "grace" or graciousness. "For the law was given by Moses, but grace and truth came by Jesus Christ." (Jn. 1:17)

When Jesus came into the world like the sunburst of God he was "full of grace and truth." Graciousness is something over and above justice. The Romans could compel any Hebrew to carry his baggage one mile. It was the law. But when Jesus admonished his followers to pick up their burden at the end of that mile and graciously carry on for yet another mile, he was introducing a new rule of conduct for which there was no precedent. Jesus' second-mile philosophy, had it been cheerfully practiced, would have changed the entire course of history for the Hebrew people. An eye for an eye was Hebrew justice but it never settled a dispute. Jesus demanded that his followers abandon such practices in favor of a more gracious way of life. We have all received so much from the hand of God and from society for which we can never pay except by giving ourselves and our substance joyously and graciously over and above the demands of justice. "Freely ye have received, freely give." (Matt. 10:8)

We accept life from our parents as a gift for which they have labored and sacrificed and suffered, a gift we have not earned and which we can never repay. In the hospital where we are born are doctors to serve us who are debtors to all the daring pioneers in medical history. The hospital itself is a marvelous repository of the gifts of countless numbers of people to which we could hardly lay the slightest claim.

The clothes we wear, the homes we live in, the public conveyances that carry us from place to place all stem back into a remote past made possible by the inventions and sacrifices of our ancestors. Walk into any public library and look around. There on the shelves are countless volumes containing the thought and history of the human race in every conceivable field. It is instantly at our disposal without cost.

Back of our cherished freedoms of the press, of speech, of assembly, and of worship we find a Paul Revere on his famous midnight ride, a Washington at Valley Forge or a gaunt Lincoln on his knees praying for the preservation of the Union. We find tens of thousands of our finest boys in premature graves in two World Wars in order that we may live on in possession of our cherished freedoms. Dare any man say that justice demands that he be given this priceless heritage because it is his due? Or is it all a marvelous gift of God and man for which we can never, never pay? "Freely ye have received, freely give." There is indeed a sound basis for Jesus' second-mile philosophy of life.

Every church roll has upon it the names of honest, punctilious, law-abiding but solemn and hard-hearted members who are quite devoid of compassion or graciousness toward their fellows. Any breech of the code they have grimly set themselves to live by is met by a joyless mouth with the lips set in a long thin line and the flash of a gimlet eye that bores you through and through. Far from winning the errant friend into paths of rectitude they tend to drive him into the other direction. Men can be drawn toward the good life by a radiant and gracious personality but they cannot be driven into the Kingdom of God by a joyless and pious fraud.

"The merely pious ministers are very empty, and deserve all that has been heaped upon them of contempt through the ages," said Bishop Phillips Brooks in his Yale Lectures on Preaching in 1877. "They are cheats and shams. As they stand with their little knobs of prejudice down their straight çoats of precision, they are like nothing so much as the chest of drawers which Mr. Bob Sawyer showed to Mr. Winkle in his surgery: 'Dummies, my dear boy,' said he to his impressed, astonished visitor; 'half the drawers have nothing in them, and the other half don't open.' "

And how the gracious word and the generous act spreads the oil of gladness on the troubled waters of our daily human contacts! It was an Englishman, met in a train somewhere in Europe, who startled Mark Twain by saying abruptly, "Mr. Clemens, I would give ten pounds not to have read your *Huckleberry Finn!*" And when the astonished author arched an inquisitive eyebrow in the direction of the maker of this puzzling remark, the Englishman smiled and added: "So that I could have again the great pleasure of reading it for the first time."

Mothers-in-law have such rare opportunities to go beyond the demands of justice as one of our young married women found to her great delight. On an extended honeymoon the young husband had often remarked that he hoped his bride might some day be able to bake the kind of muffins his mother made. The evening that they arrived for their first visit in the husband's home, his mother saw the anxious look on the bride's face as the young man sniffed expectantly around the oven and repeated his fond hope. As that mother set some burned muffins on the table she confided in her new daughter: "I did it on purpose; he should have known better!"

It was reported in a Chicago paper recently that one Richard Cromwell, told to pay his wife twenty dollars a week alimony, surprised the judge by protesting that he did not think it was enough. Still more shocked when he heard the estranged wife say she was sure it was more than she needed, the judge said, "You two are still in love—divorce not granted." I wondered whether the judge admonished them to use the gracious word next time *before* landing in the divorce court!

One recalls, in this connection, the remarkable record of Jane Carlyle as, without much outward appreciation from her brilliant but dyspeptic husband, she tried to keep the domestic waters smooth for the flowering of his genius. In the nave of the abbey kirk at Haddington you may read this inscription over her grave: "In her bright existence she had more sorrows than are common but also a soft invincibility, a capacity of discernment, and a noble heart which are rare. For forty years she was the true and loving helpmate of her husband, and by act and word unweariedly forwarded him as none else could in all of worthy that he did or attempted. She died at London, 21st April, 1866, suddenly snatched from him, and the light of his life is as if gone out."

What a tragedy that Thomas Carlyle did not fully appreciate this remarkable woman while she lived! How like many of the rest of us he was in his failure to give her the gracious word of appreciation while she lived instead of waiting to write it on her tombstone. Soon after her death, Carlyle visited her grave and read the inscription which he had placed there. If only Jane could know what he had inscribed to her! If only he had told her some of those things while she lived!

The entry which he made in his diary that night is one of the most moving bits of writing in the whole field of literature: "Cherish what is dearest while you have it near you, and wait not till it is far away. Blind and deaf that we are; oh, think, if thou yet love anybody living, wait not till death sweep down the paltry little dust clouds and dissonances of the moment, and all be at last so mournfully clear and beautiful when it is too late."

When it is too late! Alas and alas! How many millions of men and women have waited until it was too late before giving voice to some gracious overflow of the heart! Are there some of us who are waiting to write words of appreciation on some tombstone? How long, gentlemen, has it been since you said it with flowers?

Nor should we wait until we want something and thus, consciously or unconsciously, have an ulterior motive for our gracious act. Driving through the Shenandoah Valley last summer, some tourists stopped at a high point of entrancing beauty to enjoy the scenery. Several twelve-year-old boys had fruit stands near by. One of these lads smilingly approached our tourist friends and offered the use of his binoculars. He also passed a plate of red shiny apples around. When asked what they owed him he shook his curly head: "Nothing at all; it is so beautiful here that I enjoy seeing other people enjoy it—and the fruit is free. It's so beautiful. . . ."

After each of the stunned seekers had tipped the lad a quarter, they asked how he could afford to give away his time and his fruit when the other boys near by were all making a charge. He grinned as he pulled out a handful of quarters: "I am making a lot more than they are," he said. They smiled but they saw straight through our "generous" young friend.

A gracious heart that gives selflessly because it loves is a redemptive force of incomparable power. Do you recall the depraved condition of mind and soul of Jean Valjean in Hugo's *Les Misérables* as he approached the bishop's hospitable home? Nineteen years of brutal treatment in the galleys for stealing a loaf of bread for his starving family had so hardened his attitude toward all men that he seemed hopelessly lost. Driven fearfully away from every inn that he approached, he was nearly exhausted when he sought food and shelter for the night from the old bishop.

At supper time, he noticed the silver plate and candlesticks and made careful note of where the housekeeper put them after the meal. Then, in the dead of night, he stole the plates and slipped quietly over the wall and into the open country. When four gendarmes brought him back to the bishop's house: "Ah, there you are!" smiled the bishop. "I am glad to see you. But! I gave you the candlesticks also, which are silver like the rest, and would bring two hundred francs. Why did you not take them along with the plates?"

It is little wonder that Victor Hugo says that no tongue could describe the look of astonishment and relief on Jean Valjean's face. After the police had gone the bishop said: "Forget not, never forget that you have promised me to use this silver to become an honest man." Jean Valjean could recall no such promise but the bishop continued: "Jean Valjean, my brother: You belong no longer to evil but to good. It is your soul that I am buying for you. I withdraw it from dark thoughts and from the spirit of perdition, and I give it to God!"

As he wandered off through the countryside the poor benumbed and besotted soul had no idea of becoming a good man. When Petit Gervais dropped his forty-sou piece and it rolled near the stone on which Jean Valjean was resting, he put his heavy boot on it and kept it there until he had driven the sobbing child away. It was then that the vision of the saintly bishop came back to him in contrast to the beastly character of a man who could rob a weeping child of a forty-sou piece.

Hugo's description of the turmoil of this penitent man's soul is one of the most penetrating pieces of writing in literature:

His conscience weighed in turn these two men thus placed before it, the bishop and Jean Valjean. By one of those singular effects which are peculiar to this kind of ecstasy, as his reverie continued, the bishop grew grander and more resplendent in his eyes; Jean Valjean shrank and faded away. At one moment, he was but a shadow. Suddenly he disappeared. The bishop alone remained. He filled the whole soul of this wretched man with a magnificent radiance.

Victor Hugo then concludes his chapter with this deep insight into the soul struggle of a man who has set his foot on the road to the complete transformation which one gracious act had begun for him:

Jean Valjean wept long. . . . While he wept the light grew brighter and brighter in his mind—an extraordinary light, a light at once transporting and terrible. His past life, his first offense, his long expiation, his brutal exterior, his hardened exterior, his release made glad by so many schemes of vengeance, what had happened to him at the bishop's, his last action, this theft of forty sous from a child, a crime meaner and the more monstrous that it came after the bishop's pardon, all this returned and appeared to him, clearly, but in a light that he had never seen before. He beheld his life, and it seemed to him horrible; his soul, and it seemed to him frightful. There was, however, a softened light upon that life and upon that soul. It seemed to him that he was looking upon Satan by the light of Paradise.

The last glimpse which Hugo gives us of our tortured friend that night, about three o'clock in the morning, he is kneeling upon the pavement in front of the bishop's house in the attitude of prayer. Does this story not throw a ray of brilliant light across a rugged, splintered cross on which a lowly carpenter from Nazareth once hung? And is not the redemptive force that still streams from that cross the result of the most gracious and selfless act which the world has ever known? "Freely ye have received, freely give!"

 ## THE SIN AGAINST THE FUTURE

In the year 520 B.C. the prophet Zechariah went to bed one night with something pressing on his mind and heart with such urgency that he was disturbed by a vivid dream. His people had been exiled for many years in far-away Babylonia, but now, with the consent of Cyrus the Persian conqueror, they were returning home in large numbers. Zechariah was consumed with a brilliant vision for rebuilding the broken, crumbling city of Jerusalem along lines that far surpassed anything the city had ever known.

But what did he find? He found that the great majority of the returned exiles were possessed by a deep despair; that the surrounding tribes were hostile, crops bad, and that religious indifference and skepticism filled the air; that the daring creative spirit with an eye on a glorious future was in almost total eclipse. It was his concern for the future that caused Zechariah to toss restlessly and dream fitfully on that night in the long ago.

He dreamed that he saw a man with a measuring line in his hand. When Zechariah asked him where he was going he replied, "To measure Jerusalem, to see what is the breadth thereof, and what is the length thereof." Then appeared two angels, one of which said to the other, "Run, speak to this young man, saying, Jerusalem shall be inhabited as towns without walls for the multitude of men and cattle there in; for I, said the Lord, will be unto her a wall of fire round about, and will be the glory in the midst of her. Not by might nor by power, but by my spirit, saith the Lord of hosts."

The young man with the measuring line was sinning against the future. He contemplated building the new Jerusalem along the small, cramped lines of the old destroyed mountain fortress. He had no vision, no faith, no daring. He did not believe in the God who wanted a city built without confining walls; a God who would be a wall of fire round about men of faith and vision; a God who could not help a man who sinned against the future because of the great negation of his spirit.

After twenty-five hundred years this story still hits us with titanic force because we are still sinning against the future. I am just now reading one of the most challenging books that it has ever been my good fortune to acquire—Overstreet's *The Mature Mind*. The author proves beyond the shadow of a doubt that the great preponderance of people are immature in their mental processes, forever striving to solve adult problems by bringing to bear the immature judgments of children. To do this is to sin against the future.

The difficulty is, you see, that most people suffer from arrested development or fixation. The great contribution of psychology and psychiatry of recent years has been the discovery of why this is true. They tell us that whenever, in the formative years of life, an intense emotional conflict is left unresolved, it does not disappear but remains as a festering element in the unconscious mind. Instead of going on to maturity, the individual's understanding becomes fixated at that childish level and remains there until that conflict is discovered and eradicated.

For example, if early in life a child learns that he can get what he wants by making a nuisance of himself, by screaming, kicking, holding his breath and generally having a tantrum, he experiences a conflict between his selfish desires and those of his wiser parents. A "mature" solution of the problem would involve a mutual talking out of the situation and an explanation of the fact that the child is living in a society where "others-mindedness" must be developed in the place of self-centeredness if we would be happy and successful persons.

If, however, this conflict is not resolved and unwise parents continue to give in to our problem child, he is very apt to have his development fixed at that point. At forty he will still be having tantrums; browbeating his wife; terrifying his children; bawling out his subordinates. The immature mind is egocentric and predominantly negative and without faith. The characteristic of the mature mind, on the other hand, is that it is sociocentric or others-minded; it *affirms life* by becoming involved heart and soul, with faith, in the living process.

The life and teaching of Jesus of Nazareth is the greatest power and force the world has ever seen for causing men to stop being children and to grow up into robust maturity. When he commands us to love God and other men with *all* the heart, mind, soul and strength, he is saying, "Stop being self-centered and childish and negative and begin now, by a daring act of faith, to *affirm* life through your personal relationship to the God of all Creation."

Such mature people are *kind*. When Albert Schweitzer was in America recently he quoted Goethe as having said that "the supreme manifestation of the human spirit is kindness." Let us stop right there for a moment. How this poor old world has suffered for the lack of just a little kindness in these last terrible decades! And how supremely great and utterly mature was the judgment of Christ on those who put him to death when he cried, "Father, forgive them, for they know not what they do!" He was calling them childish and immature in their lack of comprehension of the enormity of their crime. Likewise he called the man who filled his barns and neglected his soul "stupid," immature; and the five maidens who neglected to fill their lamps with oil for the wedding were "foolish." They were all sinners against the future because they were facing adult problems with the immature and egocentric minds of children. Jesus was the kindest man that ever lived because his love was greater than that of any other.

A new world is struggling to be born in which the basic number is "one," one world, one people, one economy, one church, one government. The old racial, religious, cultural and nationalistic antagonism of the past must go and go soon if we are to avoid total self-annihilation in atomic war.

We are undoubtedly making progress toward World Government with one economy but there are still too many immature and childish minds sinning against the future by giving voice to one negation after another.

We sin against the future when we refuse to reëxamine our childhood faith in the interests of more inclusive and mature conceptions. Here is a case in point in an anonymous letter that came to my desk a few days ago. It came on beautiful stationery with a border of pink roses and with bluebirds of happiness flying in and out among the flowers:

REV. DUNNINGTON: (No "dear" in that salutation.)

My forefathers were all Methodists. So I grew up in and joined the Methodist Church and married a Methodist minister's son. We started our son in the Methodist Church and were perfectly happy and contented with our choice. Upon moving to Iowa City a few years ago we started attending the Methodist Church. But we were *shocked* when we heard you say: It is not a matter of importance in your religious life whether you believe in the virgin birth of Jesus or not. From that minute we were finished with the Methodist Church of Iowa City for it is an insult to fundamental religion and to Methodism to say such a thing. I am a child of God and I wish to discard no part of the Bible.

She signed it, "One who is praying for you."

I hope I may not seem irreverent if I remark that here is a situation that calls for less prayer and more honest and mature consideration of the facts with the *mind* that Jesus advised us all to use when we worship God. What I said in brief was this: Matthew and Luke who tell the beautiful story of the virgin birth of Jesus also give a lot of clear evidence that Joseph was the father of Jesus. Matthew 1:16 says, in tracing Jesus' lineage back to David: "And Jacob begat Joseph the husband of Mary, of whom was born Jesus, who is called Christ." And Luke 3:23 says: "And Jesus himself began to be about thirty years of age, being (as was supposed) the son of Joseph," and thence traces the lineage back to David and finally to Adam.

In one chapter on the virgin birth in *Something to Stand On* we give much other evidence from the New Testament to the same effect and conclude that the Bible therefore gives two choices to anybody. You may believe in the virgin birth or you may disbelieve in the virgin birth and cite equally good scripture to prove your point.

My own conclusion is, therefore, that nobody will ever know for sure whether Jesus was virgin born but that, in any case, it is not an important element of one's Christian faith. The Bible nowhere says that you *must* believe it; neither Jesus nor any of his disciples ever so much as mentioned it; and where and how Jesus got his *body* would not seem to have any bearing one way or another on where and how he came to possess his God-filled soul.

My lady correspondent (I can't imagine a man going for all those bluebirds on the border) is undoubtedly a very devout and sincere Christian. But she is immature in her determination to stick to childhood beliefs in the face of new evidence and in her petulant decision to drop out of our church forever instead of courageously coming to her minister for a quiet talk and more light. It is that childish spirit that has caused over two hundred and fifty denominational divisions to weaken our Protestant forces at a time when we need to heed Paul's call for "One Lord, one faith, one baptism, one God and Father of all, who is above all, and through all, and in you all."

I am reminded of the wisdom and insight of William Penn, the Quaker who suffered so grievously from the vicious persecution of certain churchmen of his day: "A devout man is one thing, a stickler is another. To be furious in religion is to be irreligiously religious. It were better to be of no church, than to be bitter for any . . . *nor can spirits ever be divided that love and live in the same Divine principle.*"

We sin against the future when we give voice to frustration and despair because our lot has not fallen in more pleasant places. We forget that our very words have power to create either good or ill and that *our unconscious minds must accept what our conscious minds dwell upon and bring that into manifestation.*

People who face their problems with mature minds and hearts, who, in spite of difficulty and even tragedy, immerse themselves gladly in the stream of life with faith and hope and love, with life's great affirmations breaking through every decision, little realize how much they are doing by their very example to bring in a brighter future. Let a veteran tell his experience in his own words:

"I was a veteran going to the university. My wife and I were unable to find adequate housing and finally ended up in a worn-out, dirty, little cottage with almost no plumbing. My checks had been delayed. A baby was on the way. It seemed to me that we were as miserable as we could get. My courses were stiff, but between classes I tried to find a more livable apartment.

"Martha had always had a large, luxurious home; it was hard for her to live in poverty. Often she was fretful, and in spite of myself I would get into stupid arguments with her. It was after a particularly silly argument one morning that I went to the veteran's advisor and told him that I had decided to drop out of school and get a job.

" 'You've got less than a year to go for your degree,' he told me.

" 'I know it, but we can't go on this way any longer,' I said irritably.

"He listened attentively and sympathetically while I explained my problems—griped about the housing situation, high cost of living and the other things that beset a veteran trying to finish his schooling.

"I noticed that his glance often went to a picture on his desk as he listened to my outpourings, and a little later when the phone rang and he was called out of the office I took a look at the picture. It was a picture of a girl with great, dark eyes and a tranquil smile.

" 'He's a lucky guy,' I muttered. 'Nice wife, good job, probably got a big home. . . .' I didn't mean to envy him but suddenly it didn't seem fair.

"He returned while I was staring at the picture.

" 'Your wife?' I asked, startled at his entrance.

" 'Yes.' I noticed that his eyes became a little misty.

" 'Well, you sure picked yourself a honey.'

" 'She was a wonderful girl,' he replied, sitting down and lighting his pipe, his voice was suddenly husky. I sank back into my chair; I felt all at once like a heel.

" 'She died last year,' he continued.

" 'I'm sorry,' I muttered.

" 'That's all right.' His voice was quiet. 'Perhaps it might help you to hear about her. She was a wonderful person.' He told me that they had married during the war and she worked in Washington while he was overseas. 'Not having a strong constitution, overworking in her job and helping community organizations she contracted tuberculosis. She went out west to a sanatorium until I came back on leave. She had improved and I was sure that she would get well. After thirty days I had to return to my station in Europe. It was our last good-bye. I think she must have known that we would not meet again on earth, because there was something angelic about her, an ethereal softness, when I left her. Before I went she asked me whether I would object if she gave her eyes to some blind person when she died. She had heard about a plan which allowed a person to sign a paper. At death the cornea of your eyes would then be transplanted to another. It was just like her. She was always thinking of a way to help others, although always unobtrusively.' He cleared his throat. 'Well, when I was on my way back home, she died,' he said quietly. 'And upon her death, a blind man was operated on and given sight with her cornea.'

"There wasn't anything for me to say. I thought of the comparatively simple problems that confronted my wife and me, and I felt deeply ashamed that I had let them get me down.

" 'She must have been a brave woman,' I got out finally.

" 'She was one of the courageous ones,' he replied. 'Now and then it helps us to know that people can face life so bravely.'

" 'Just stick with it, things will work out,' the advisor told me.

" 'Thank you sir,' I said, then quickly left the office. As I shut the door, I glanced at him. He was looking at his wife's picture, and on his face was a sad but serene expression that told of the strength of his spirit.

" 'Another of the courageous ones,' I thought as I went toward my classes."

 ## THE FORGIVING GOD

Let us take for granted the awful fact of a world full of sinful men. With books, magazines and newspapers devoting themselves so largely to depicting the stories of man's inhumanity to man we shall need not a single paragraph on it. What we do need to discuss, however, is our attitude toward the wrongdoer. Where lies the wise course of action that has within it the great redempting power? Assuming that we are deeply concerned with rectifying situations involving injustice, hatred and selfishness in human relations, what can we do about it?

The captain of a ship once wrote in his log, "Mate was drunk all day." When the mate sobered up, he pleaded with the captain to delete that line. He reminded his superior officer of the fact that he had never been drunk before. The captain was unforgiving and adamant. "In this log," he said, "we write the exact truth and nobody is ever allowed to change it." The next week when the mate kept the log he wrote: "The captain has been cold-sober now for two days." Nor would he change "the truth" even though the captain had never been drunk in his life!

The mate's attitude was a normal reaction to a hard-boiled captain. Jesus revealed God's attitude toward erring men when he said: "You have heard that it was said, 'Thou shalt love thy neighbor and hate thine enemy.' But I command you all, love your enemies, and pray for your persecutors; *so that you may become true sons of your Father in Heaven;* for He causes His sun to rise on the wicked as well as the good, and sends rain upon those who do right and those who do wrong." (Matt. 5:43–45—Weymouth trans.)[1]

When Jesus told the matchless story of the Prodigal Son, the watching and critical Pharisees were sure, as they listened to the first part of the story, that the boy would be lost. The Prodigal himself at one time felt irrevocably lost. His friends, his character, his reputation, his inner controls were gone, and in the courtroom of his own soul he had passed the sentence of "guilty" upon himself. One chance only remained. If his old father still loved him, and if he returned in penitence, perhaps the old gentleman would take him back as a hired-hand. So, turning his back on the swine, he headed for home, and "while he was yet afar off" a forgiving father opened his arms. That father's pardon could not remove from the boy's life the fearful consequences of his sin. As long as he lived, the scars on his health, reputation and usefulness would be there. But forgiveness could restore the old relationships of mutual confidence and love; and the fight for a new life could be waged, not in a far and hostile country, but at home. *And God is like that father,* said Jesus.

Those who have the Father's loving and forgiving spirit within them act the way God would act. Not what they *say* but what they *do* constitutes the yardstick by which we are to measure them. When, by God's help, we rise to character's mountain-top to act like true sons of God; when we truly understand and forgive, we start an ennobling influence sweeping down the corridors of time whose final outcome only God can foresee.

Look at Stephen. Beaten to his knees by the savage mob, the blood pouring from the stone-gouged wounds in his face, the great soul

[1] *Weymouth's New Testament in Modern Speech.* Published by Harper & Brothers. Used by permission.

dared to pray God to "lay not this sin to their charge." Paul was standing there with folded arms watching Stephen's face. It reflected the ineffable light of heaven; and that prayer! Whoever heard of anything like *that?* It was not too long afterward that Paul, persecuting all Christians to the death, felt the impact of Stephen's prayer in the blinding light that struck him on the Damascus Road. The forgiving God found reflection in the forgiving Christ of the Cross, thence through Stephen to Paul and—who would dare try to estimate the breadth and depth of that stream of influence down the ages?

We have heard much of late of chain-reaction in releasing atomic power. But here is the chain-reaction that goes on redemptively to the end of time. Jesus must have been thinking of this when, after Peter asked him how often he should forgive a brother who kept on sinning against him, he answered, "I say not unto thee until seven times: but until seventy times seven."

Is that not the attitude of God towards every one of us? How often do we resolve to live with Him more closely; to talk with Him in prayer many times a day; and how often do we allow the trite affairs of this world to crowd Him out! How patient He is! How forgiving! Let us be assured that no matter what we do He will never let us go. Like Francis Thompson's "Hound of Heaven," He is forever on our trail, seeking us.

How great a soul it takes to forgive like God! Do you remember that amazing episode in Leonardo da Vinci's life when he forgave that way? He had just entered the inner courtyard of the Castle of Milan one day when his attention was arrested by a group of soldiers gesticulating and talking wildly in front of his great Colossus. He was horrified to learn that there was soon to be an arrow-shooting contest. A German and a Frenchman were about to drink four mugs of wine apiece and then shoot at the wart on the nose of the Colossus.

Leonardo was frozen to the spot with horror. About to be destroyed was the creation of the sixteen best years of his life—the greatest work of sculpture since the time of Phidias in the Golden Age of Greece. The Great Duke, the conqueror of Lombardy, Francesco Attendolo Sforza, with an expression of leonine power, sat as of yore, on his magnificent steed, that reared up on its hind legs and trampled a fallen warrior with its hoofs. Yes, the Colossus was world famous. The German drained off his wine, pulled up and shot—and missed.

Not so the Frenchman. His cruel arrow cut straight through the wart and ruined that magnificent head. Other shots followed from the drunken revelers and presently the Colossus lay in ruins. At that moment, the chief military commander of the French king passed through the square and, aghast at the destruction of France's most cherished work of art, grabbed the guilty men and would have run them through with his sword had not Leonardo da Vinci grabbed the flashing blade. "Monseigneur, I beseech you, be not wroth—forgive them," said the artist; "even if you were to hang them all, what would that avail me or my creation? They know not what they do." There was an artist bigger than his work. That was one of the most Godlike requests ever made by man.

There has been much of that same forgiving spirit in the record of our Japanese-American G.I.'s in the late war. The 100th Infantry Battalion was made up almost entirely of American citizens of Japanese ancestry, many of them having come straight out of the Relocation Centers. Some of them could write a book on the injustices from which they suffered in the days following Pearl Harbor. The average American simply lost his head and his reason in his anti-Japanese fury. Yet those boys forgave us and became the most decorated unit in the history of the U.S. Army. Its 1,300 members have been awarded more than 1,000 Purple Hearts, 73 Silver Stars, 96 Bronze Stars, 21 Distinguished Service Crosses, 6 Legion-of-Merit medals and 16 Division citations. They landed at Salerno, spearheaded the Fifth Army advances, held the front at Cassino for forty days and led the break-through on Rome. In the three years of the battalion's existence, there was not one desertion or even an absence of one hour without leave! They are proud of two cases of A.W.O.L. —in reverse—wounded soldiers who got up from their hospital beds to rejoin their unit when it moved on. They fought that way to prove that they loved America with all their hearts in spite of what had happened to them. The America of tomorrow will not forget this spirit of forgiveness.

The true forgiving spirit cannot be a halfway matter. It must be all-out. Jesus put into his famous prayer, "Forgive us our trespasses *as we forgive* those who trespass against us." God's forgiving spirit toward us is dependent on our forgiving spirits. They are inextricably tied in together. When we forgive, God does!

Andrew Jackson found this out. When, in his retirement, the old warrior was about to join the church and the minister was examining his faith, he was asked: "General can you forgive all your enemies?" The question was relative to the many feuds, duels, and personal bitternesses in Jackson's stormy career. After a moment's silence, Jackson responded: "My political enemies I can freely forgive; but as for those who abused me when I was serving my country in the field, and those who attacked me for serving my country, and those who slandered my wife . . . Doctor, that is a different case."

The minister then made it clear to the old warrior that none who wilfully harbored ill feelings against a fellow being could make a sincere profession of faith—*That God forgives us as we forgive others*. Again there was a short silence when at length the aged candidate affirmed that he would try to forgive *all* of his enemies. This done his name was entered in the roll of the church.

It is a pity that as valiant a soul as Andy Jackson could not have learned more about the power of forgiveness earlier in life. His stormy career could have been so much more calm. Forgiveness and the generous attitude toward one who has done wrong often wins him to paths of rectitude where all else fails. Roswell McIntyre deserted during the Civil War; he was caught, court-martialled and condemned to death. The lad did not try to defend his act nor did he complain concerning the awful penalty that the court wished to exact. He did say that if he were to have another chance, he felt he could play the man. On that basis, President Lincoln pardoned him: "Upon condition that Roswell McIntyre of Co. E, 6th Reg't. of New York Cavalry, returns to his regiment and faithfully serves out his term, making up for lost time, or until otherwise discharged, he is fully pardoned for any supposed desertion heretofore committed, and this paper is his pass to go to his regiment."

President Lincoln was often criticized for his generous and forgiving spirit. Was such clemency an occasion for lax character? Very seldom. In this case the answer is written across the face of the President's letter and may be found in the archives: "Taken from the body of R. McIntyre at the Battle of Five Forks, Va., 1865." Five Forks was the last cavalry battle of the Civil War; McIntyre went on through to the finish!

There is not the slightest reason to limit the redemptive power of forgiveness to this life. Jesus said that the Kingdom of heaven or of spirit was like a grain of mustard seed. It contains the principle of endless unfoldment and growth—both here and over there. And since we shall all enter that other world imperfect and in need of forgiveness, there is every reason to believe that its blessed benefits will accrue to us over there. After Jesus returned from the tomb on Easter morning, who was the first man he singled out for special attention? Peter! "Tell my disciples—*and tell Peter,* I go before you into Galilee." Why Peter? Because Peter was in the greatest need of the Master's forgiveness. Had he not denied Jesus three times on that blackest of all Friday nights? And had he not spent considerable time of late assuring Jesus of his love and constancy? Ah, yes! Tell my disciples—but especially tell Peter; he will know he is forgiven!

In "The Ballad of Judas Iscariot," Robert Buchanan gives us a glimpse of the inexhaustible power of this spirit as it spans two worlds. He describes the soul of Judas after he has taken his own life, lost and desolate, yet unable to die. The light will not shine on him. The very elements loathe him. Hell has no place for him. At last, in utter loneliness and despair, he sees a small light far away. He crawls toward it over the moor. It shines from a cabin window and inside Jesus sits at the table with the eleven. The Master asks them whose weary feet he hears outside. He is told that a wolf is probably running up and down in the snow. Again he asks who it is that must be shivering out there in the dark. There is a fierce answer: it is the soul of Judas Iscariot "gliding to and fro." He takes a light and holds it in his hand. Then:

> 'Twas the Bridegroom stood at the open door,
> And beckoned, smiling sweet,
> 'Twas the soul of Judas Iscariot
> Stole in, and fell at his feet.
> The Holy Supper is spread within,
> And the many candles shine,
> And I have waited long for thee
> Before I poured the wine.

I like Buchanan's thought there. It is so like the forgiving Christ. He promised the repentant thief on the cross to see him that very Friday afternoon on the other side of the river of death. There was so much that needed to be said to the thief whose feet were now planted

in a new road, a road that climbed slowly upward toward the Eternal
City of God.

So, why not Judas also? Sobbing bitterly and utterly broken-hearted
and repentant over the awful sin of having sold his Master for thirty
pieces of silver, Judas had stumbled blindly back to the scene of his
crime and hurled the silver to the floor at the feet of the High Priest
as he cried, "I have betrayed the innocent blood." Then he had hung
himself.

On the other side of the line of worlds that afternoon, therefore,
Jesus must have encountered two repentant men, the thief and Judas.
Is there any reason to believe that the one would have received any
more loving, forgiving attention from Jesus than the other? I cannot
think so. Redemption is conditioned upon one thing alone—re-
pentance—whether here or over there. The God that Jesus portrayed
is not interested in punishment except as a remedial agent. Such
suffering as Judas experienced comes from within ourselves because
we have been made in God's own image and when we have repented,
God instantly takes us back into fellowship with Himself. God's attitude toward his children must be the same over there as here.

Wouldn't you like to have heard the conversation that took place
between Jesus and Judas on Good Friday night?

 ## LIGHT AND SHADOW

The most satisfying landscapes are a combination of light
and shadow. They belong together. We could not have the
one without the other. Light is life-giving but sometimes it shines so
brightly that we seek the shade for a respite from the heat. I love
that great line in Isaiah (32:2): "And a man shall be as an hiding
place from the wind . . . as the shadow of a great rock in a weary
land."

An interesting and worthwhile life is always a combination of light
and shadow. Without that contrast we should find the business of
living insipid and distasteful. What would the life of Christ be without the dark and ominous shadows of his last week on earth? We do
not mean to suggest that God planned it that way. In a world of

free choice there are bound to develop forces that put good men to the most severe tests. But would we ever know how great and strong a person could be unless he had been put to the test? Was it not Gethsemane and the cross that gave us the real Christ? Is there a comparable event in all the history of the world that so revealed to man the compassion and love and understanding of God?

There is a hymn that reads:

> Our years are like the shadows
> The sunny hills that lie.

Indeed, they are; a good deal of light relieved by plenty of shadow. And each has its place. At least I shall continue to think so until somebody comes along who can show me one strong, interesting life without shadows. Then I shall of necessity revise my whole concept of the place of Jesus in the lives of men.

Helen Keller has said: "The one resolution, which was in my mind long before it took the form of a resolution, *is the keynote of my life*. It is this: always to regard as mere impertinence of fate the handicaps which were placed upon my life almost at the beginning. *I resolved that they should not crush or dwarf my soul, but rather be made to blossom like Aaron's rod with flowers*." The ominous shadows of blindness, deafness and dumbness were the very ingredients which, because of what her indomitable soul did with them, produced a personality of rare radiance and charm.

Some day I should like to write a book about the men who owed their lasting contributions to the race to some unhappy adventure of health or fortune, some catastrophe of banishment or imprisonment, wherein, having mastered their own souls, they were able to give the world a priceless heritage.

Paul wrote some of his best letters from Roman jails and did some of his most lusty singing at midnight behind prison bars. It was in Bedford Gaol that John Bunyon wrote *Pilgrim's Progress* and then doubted whether he should have it printed. "I did it," he says, "my own self to gratify." This best seller of all time next to the Bible itself would never have been composed but for the shadow of a jail.

William Penn, the Quaker, founder of the City of Brotherly Love, wrote *Some Fruits of Solitude* while banished from the court. He speaks of solitude as "a school few care to learn in, though none in-

structs us better." He "blesseth God for His retirement. He has now
some Time he could call his own; in which he has taken a View of
himself and the World; and observed wherein he hath hit and missed
the mark." Such results make one wonder whether a sentence of
banishment might not be a good thing once in a while for all of us.
But then again, it would all depend on what we did with it. It is not
the shadow but our use of it that counts.

That is what David Grayson wrote from the prison-house of a bed
of illness. He asked himself how one could lie watching forever the
angle of light that came through the half-open door? Anything was
better than that. He would get up and walk out. But misery, he truly
told himself, is not physical but mental. *It is what we think, not what
we suffer that destroys us; and that man is successful who has learned
to live triumphantly within his limitations.*

One morning David Grayson faced himself squarely. Out of all of
the overflowing experiences of a busy life was there nothing left to
carry him through a few months in bed? Had he no resources of
spirit? Just because his health, books, friends and work had been
suddenly swept away for a while, did that mean he was helpless? No!
It did not! He still had his own mind and his own inner life. Only
this strange something deep within could bring him peace and comfort.

Thus when he awakened in the night, it was no longer to the bored
misery of former nights. He began adventuring in the realm of mind
and spirit, telling himself that adventure is not outside man but
within. There one meets himself and his God and finds tranquillity
through the good ordering of the mind.

There are some of you who are reading these words who have read
David Grayson's *Great Possessions, The Friendly Road* and *Adventures in Solitude* and you may be saying: "Yes, we expect that of
him. He was a great soul with extraordinary inner resources. But
some of us have seen the shadows deepen into the inky blackness of
midnight and despair."

In Portland, Oregon, in a bed in room 38 of the Portland General
Hospital, lies a remarkable woman who has adventured much through
light and shadow. She is Mary Leona McKay or just "Mary Leona
of the Seven Open Windows" as multitudes call her. One lung is
collapsed because of T.B. so the windows are kept open. She coughs

with cardiac asthma, has had two strokes because of high blood pressure and cataracts on both eyes impair her vision. "By all the rules," she jokes, "I should have been dead long ago." Any one of her thousands of Portland friends, however, will tell you that her unquenchable faith and contagious happiness fill her life with such radiant light that the shadows never have a chance.

Before she was taken ill, Miss McKay was superintendent of the junior and intermediate leagues in a Methodist Church in a Portland suburb. Whenever there is a marriage among them the whole wedding party troops over to the room of the Seven Open Windows for a hilarious send-off from one they love. For more than eleven years a group has been coming every Sunday to swap yarns and sing. When illness prevents her seeing them they send cards "To our Mother, from the Gang." And from that room she heads up many a philanthropic movement in the city to help the poor and unfortunate.

On a typewriter balanced on the bed in front of her she has written four books, one of which she calls *Adventures Within Four Walls*— a volume that has brought inspiration and help to thousands of the world's sufferers. Because, you see, she never cries, she laughs; she never scolds, she counsels with deep sympathy and understanding; she never complains as she struggles against terrifying odds.

How does she do it? Through her vital faith in the Living God. She keeps her mind turned away from trouble toward the joy, light and love of God. She keeps that mind off of self by keeping it focussed on others. Yes, Mary Leona of the Seven Open Windows really enjoys the business of living as she helps others through the shadows into the light.

That is what Christ has been doing for millions through the centuries. He took a pious, smug selfrighteous Pharisee like Paul; a young man with no light or joy in his religion; an individual with hard set face who believed that salvation came to men as a result of the meticulous keeping of every item in the law—and showed him a vision of such resplendent light on the Damascus Road that he was henceforth completely changed.

From that day Paul had a perspective of life that properly evaluated all trouble in the light of the eternal love of God through Christ. "Who shall separate us from the love of Christ?" he cried. "Shall tribulation, or distress, or persecution, or famine, or nakedness, or

peril, or sword?—Nay, in all these things we are more than con-
querors through him that loved us." (Romans 8:35) That is the true
perspective for seeing trouble.

When the night is dark and hope and faith are dim, all we can do
is to pray and hang on. *In such darkness we should never make a
major decision.* We should wait until the morning light has driven
away the shadows and our minds and emotions are clear and fresh.

I do not know what time of day it was when beautiful, talented
Jane Froman decided to finish her mission to the boys overseas but
I'll wager it was not at midnight. She was on the Lisbon Clipper
when it crashed, killing twenty-six and badly injuring fifteen. After
eighteen operations covering many weary months, she still found it
necessary to hobble around on crutches. But she decided she must
go back anyway and entertain her boys and fulfill her contract. So
she went hobbling over Europe on a tough schedule and did the boys
far more good than she could have done had she been well.

It is nothing to be especially proud of to do one's work when one
is well and in possession of the full equipment for the job. But to do
it in spite of great handicaps—that is the thing that really tests one's
mettle. A certain American colonel will never forget one thick,
foggy night in London. He had just had word that his son, a captain,
had been severely wounded and would be operated on at once in a
London hospital.

As he prepared to go to his son's bedside, a fog so thick that he
could not see his hand in front of him settled over the city. He was
utterly lost within a few blocks of his critically ill son. He called
out: "I am an American Army officer. My son is in St. Gregory's
hospital. Won't somebody . . ."

Then a hand reached out and took his arm and a cheery voice said,
"Come along, sir!" The stranger guided him along—left, right, left,
around a corner. A huge building loomed through the darkness.
"Here you are, sir," said the voice. The colonel thanked him and then
called back: "But how did *you* find your way?" "Easily," came the
answer. "I am blind. Got it in both eyes at Dunkirk, sir," and he was
gone.

It took the heartbreak of infantile paralysis to make a real man
out of Franklin Delano Roosevelt. At least that is the opinion of
Frances Perkins who knew him about as well as anybody. She re-

members making a trip to Albany to fight for a bill to establish a 54-hour week for women in industry. Roosevelt as a young state senator was not interested. Raised in the lap of luxury, he had no conception of the struggle the average person was having to make ends meet and get a little joy out of life. She thought him guilty of "a deafness to the hopes, fears and aspirations which are the common lot."

But after a grim bout with the helplessness that goes with infantile paralysis, "the man emerged completely warmhearted, with humility of spirit and with a deeper philosophy." His power to grow in response to the hard experiences of life was beginning to show.

Failure and heartache beshadowed Abraham Lincoln through the years. When the South finally lost the Civil War there was, therefore, no room in his great heart for recrimination. When he heard the news of Lee's surrender he said, "I hope there will be no persecution, no bloody work, after the war is over. No one need expect me to take any part in hanging or killing those men, even the worst of them . . . we must extinguish our resentments if we expect harmony and reunion. . . ." How different would the whole reconstruction period have been, had the great-souled Lincoln lived to pilot his ship of state through those difficult years!

What would you consider to be the three greatest enemies of happiness in this world, the three demons that cause more black shadows to lengthen over more lives than any others? It seems to me they are worry, boredom and self-centeredness. And of the three I should say self-centeredness is the real cause of boredom and worry. When the mind is egocentric; turned in upon itself; always asking how this or that will affect *me,* that soul is very sick indeed. It lacks the basic security, the lift and the zest that come only from turning the stream of consciousness out toward others, toward God and man, in faith and confidence and love. Worry and boredom take wings and fly away because self-centeredness has been replaced by outgoingness.

The correct use of our God-given imaging power will do much to banish loneliness and boredom and worry. "I never was bored in my life," wrote Robert Louis Stevenson. When he was too sick to work, he would lie in bed and imagine himself the leader of a great horde of cavalry—himself "turning in the saddle to look back at the whole command (some five thousand strong) following me at a hard gallop up the road out of the burning valley by moonlight." At such times he would create a whole series of vivid mental pictures of thrilling events that he would later work into his matchless stories.

Imagination is a gift we all possess but it needs to be cultivated; and if fed by the reading of good books it will grow and become a source of deep satisfaction. What treasures of the mind lie buried in all of the books of men like Stevenson, Dickens, Mark Twain or a thousand others—buried until we dig them up and make them our own.

Even when we are stricken down with some incurable but lingering illness and cannot read very many hours a day, we may still keep the stream of consciousness turned outward toward others and away from self and thus keep loneliness, boredom and worry at bay.

One day I called on a middle-aged mother who had been suffering from multiple sclerosis for ten years and was unable to move from her chair. She had watched her husband die and had bravely endured the separation as her country called her two sons into World War II. I had sat beside her when the news came that one son had been killed in action. On her table lay a poem about "Shadows" which she said mirrored her own point of view. Here it is:

We cannot think that God meant shadows to be fearsome things,
Else He would not have given us the shadow of His wings.
Nor would His tall trees by the way trace out a cool, sweet place
Where weary travelers may pause to find His soothing grace.
Nor would the shadows of the night enfold us in that tranquil rest
That falls upon the sleeping babe rocked at its mother's breast.
And though the shadows over life may seem to creep apace,
Behind the darkest one of them is His assuring face!

 ## CHOOSE LIFE

About 600 B.C. the writer of the words found in Deuteronomy 30:19 put these words into the mouth of God: "I have set before thee life and death—therefore choose life." This "terrible choice" is always before us and the tragedy is that so many of us choose death even when we think we are choosing life.

The conflict is caused by two laws at work within us—a self-regarding and an others-regarding law. Since we belong physically to the animal kingdom the instinct of physical self-preservation keeps suggesting that we follow the law of the jungle. This law decrees that the fittest to survive physically are those possessing the power to secure most efficiently the interests of self. But man is also a spirit or a living soul and the law of spirit decrees that the fittest to survive are those possessing the power to give themselves most completely in the service of others.

Paul was referring to the conflict of these laws when he wrote: "I find then a law, that, where I would do good, evil is present in me. For I delight in the law of God after the inward man: But I see another law in my members warring against the law of my mind, and bringing me into captivity to the law of sin which is in my members." (Romans 7:21–24)

We are essentially selfish and egocentric during the first few years of our lives. Children are notoriously self-regarding. But as we reach and pass through adolescence a profound change should take place. The emerging personality should become others-regarding and find joy in giving himself in the service of others. When this happens he finds that, in the realm of spirit, the more he gives the more he has; the more he forgets self, the more satisfaction and happiness that self enjoys.

This paradoxical situation was explained by Jesus in these words: "Give and it shall be given unto you, good measure, pressed down, shaken together and running over shall men give into your bosom. *For with the same measure that you use it shall be measured to you again.*" (Luke 6:38) The man who would "choose life" must, therefore, choose to be a servant of mankind as he gives himself and his substance increasingly to individuals and causes that need his support.

This law applies to nations. Rulers through the ages have thought to choose life by forcibly grabbing what belonged to their subjects only to find death at the end. Jeremiah (22:11–15) tells us that King Shallum chose this evil way and God said: "Woe unto him that buildeth his house by unrighteousness and his chambers by wrong; that useth his neighbor's service without wages, and giveth him not for his work; that saith, I will build me a wide house and large chambers, and cutteth him out windows; and it is ceiled with cedar and painted with vermillion." Then God reminds Shallum of the righteous choices of Josiah, his father: "He judged the cause of the poor and needy, then it was well with him."

Coming down to modern times we see this law at work the same as in the long ago. The other day I reread a sermon that I preached in this pulpit on November 22, 1942, in which I dared to make certain predictions based on Jesus' law of spirit . . . "for with the same measure you use it shall be measured to you again." Although the Axis powers were riding high at that moment in history, with many people believing they would win, we said that the whole moral universe was pitted against them and that they must lose. Japan had stolen Manchuria and was trying to take China and everything in the Pacific; Mussolini had begun the march toward empire by the rape of Ethiopia, and Hitler had seized nation after nation. They fell even sooner than we had dared to hope.

And where are the great empires of recent centuries; of Spain, England and the Netherlands? They have all crumbled. Yet if they had had the true interests of their subject millions at heart instead of material gain, they might have stayed on for centuries. Dr. E. Stanley Jones said of Japan that had she gone into China with altruistic motives she might have had any material gain she could have desired. Selfishness coupled with complete disregard of the rights of others has ruined individuals as well as nations through the centuries.

A good God has made a world that is overflowing with a superabundance of everything that man needs. Properly distributed there could be enough of everything for everybody. If we would but obey Jesus' law of spirit there would be peace and plenty: "Give and it shall be given you . . . for with the same measure you use it shall be measured to you again." This is the law for choosing life. That is the way one loves God with all one's heart, mind and strength and one's neighbor as one's self which, as Jesus said, is all of the law and of the prophets.

Statistically the most extraordinary speech of all times was a collection of true stories woven into a lecture called "Acres of Diamonds." The lecturer, Dr. Russell H. Conwell, repeated it six thousand times over a period of fifty years to an audience that totaled millions. It stirred gatherings in small towns as well as in the largest auditoriums in our biggest cities. It drew fees ranging from a chicken dinner to nine thousand dollars. Its net earnings could easily have given its author a bank account of five million dollars and yet he died poor and was dubbed America's penniless millionaire. The manner in which Dr. Conwell gave his fortune away illustrated the truth of Jesus' law of spirit. The more he gave the more of life's deepest satisfactions became his. With life and death before him he chose life.

The theme of "Acres of Diamonds" was that untold opportunities for service, achievement and happiness lie in our own backyards at all times if we but open our eyes to them. On a trip down the Euphrates River Dr. Conwell learned from his old Arab guide the true story of the world's richest diamond mine. It seems that there lived not far from the river Indus an old Persian by the name of Ali Hafed. He owned a large farm with orchards, grain fields, and gardens. He was a contented man. Then one day a Buddhist priest came along and told Ali Hafed all about the magic beauty of diamonds and of the fabulous power that one could wield in the world if he but possessed a diamond mine.

That night Ali Hafed could not sleep. He was a poor man now; not because he had lost his farm, but because he was discontented. So he sold his farm, placed his family with a neighbor, and set out to find a diamond mine. He wandered all over the world until he was ragged and hungry and sick. At last he stood on the shore of the bay at Barcelona when a great tidal wave came rolling in between the Pillars of Hercules. Unable to withstand the temptation, this beaten, frustrated man hurled himself into the incoming tide and sank beneath its foaming crest, never to rise again.

Meanwhile, the man who bought Ali Hafed's farm one day led his camel to the garden brook to drink. As he looked down into the water he saw a flash, and on reaching into the white sand he pulled out a black stone with a flashing eye of light. It was a diamond! He reached down again and pulled out another and another, and thus discovered the world's richest diamond mine—the diamond mine of Golconda. The Kohinoor and the Orloff of the crown jewels of England and Russia, the largest diamonds on earth, came from that mine.

The reason that story struck Dr. Conwell with such force was because it had already been so well illustrated in his own life. Raised on a poor and rocky little farm in Massachusetts, he had carried a good book wherever he went, down the furrows, to the pasture or to the barn. He utilized every spare moment to stock his mind with knowledge and wisdom. While in the Union Army during the Civil War he committed the whole of Blackstone to memory, and later, while commuting by train to and from his law offices in Boston, he learned to read five languages.

But it was a touching incident that took place during the war that had the profoundest influence on his whole after-life. His diminutive orderly, Johnnie Ring, became deeply devoted to big, fine-looking Captain Conwell. One day a surprise Confederate advance near New Berne routed his company from its position. Retreating across a river, his men fired a wooden bridge behind them.

But they had cut off escape for their orderly: Johnnie Ring had dashed back to bring the captain's sword. When he finally appeared with it and found the bridge ablaze, he tried to rush through the flames but fell into the river badly burned. Dragged out half dead, his first thought was for his Captain and his sword. He smiled to find it safe beside him, took it in his arms and died.

"When I stood over his body," Conwell said later, "and realized he had died for love of me, I made a vow that I would live, thereafter, not only my own life, but also the life of John Ring, that it might not be lost." From then on, for sixty years, Russell Conwell kept his vow and worked a double day, eight hours for Johnnie Ring and eight hours for himself. And he always kept the fateful sword hanging over the head of his bed to remind him of his vow.

One day an elderly lady visited his law office in Boston to secure legal counsel on selling a distressed church property in Lexington. He went out to view the place and to talk with the forlorn little group who were being forced to give up their beloved property where they had worshipped all their lives. "Why sell it?" asked Conwell. "Why not start over?" When they objected that the building was too far gone and money too scarce he said he would help them.

On the appointed day, he borrowed some tools and went to work. No one else showed up so he started in alone, chopping away at the front veranda. When a passing townsman asked what he was going to do, he said: "Build a new church." They fell to chatting and before he left the townsman had pledged one hundred dollars toward the new building.

That gift was the only spark Conwell needed to set a real fire raging in that town. Others joined in the work or gave more and more money until the church was built. Sundays our energetic friend preached to the people in rented rooms and finally became their minister. Soon the church was overflowing with worshippers.

Then a committee came from Philadelphia and wanted him to do a similar job there. They could offer only eight hundred dollars in salary but they did say that every time the congregation doubled they would double his salary. He accepted and six years later when his salary reached ten thousand dollars he mercifully excused the trustees from carrying their agreement any further.

One Sunday, from the many being turned away from the packed sanctuary, he rescued a bewildered little girl and saw her to a place inside. She was so grateful that she resolved to save her pennies toward a church that was big enough for all. Before long, however, she died, and her grief-stricken father brought Dr. Conwell the grand sum-total of her savings—fifty-seven cents in pennies.

The author of "Acres of Diamonds" was inspired. Here was a diamond! He took the fifty-seven cents to the owner of a ten thousand dollar lot on Broad Street and that gentleman accepted it as a down payment. In due time the lot was paid for as well as a church with the largest auditorium of that day—a church that was always full of worshippers with hungry hearts waiting to be filled with hope and new life.

One evening a lad who was working as a printer solicited Conwell's advice on the best way to get an education. "Come to me one evening a week," said the great-souled minister, "and I'll begin teaching you myself." When the boy showed up however, he had six others with him. A week later there were forty in the class and by year's end two hundred and fifty mind-hungry young people were enrolled in this informal night college. Buildings rose beside the great Temple Church and became Temple University. President Conwell lived to see more than one hundred thousand pupils take work in his school.

Similar and equally unpretentious was Conwell's founding of Philadelphia's big Samaritan Hospital. Two rented rooms, one nurse and one poor patient who needed medical aid were the humble beginnings of a work that finally included three great hospitals—Samaritan, Good-heart and Garretson—in the industrial heart of the great city, and all affiliated with Temple Church and Temple University.

Through all of the ceaseless activity surrounding the maintenance of these institutions throbbed the great heart of their dynamic founder working sixteen hours a day. In addition he wrote thirty-seven volumes—biographies, travel and legal books—and gave over eight thousand lectures, usually "Acres of Diamonds."

When he was thirty-three and far from rich the author of that lecture determined to give all future returns to students fighting the kind of material odds and social discrimination that he himself had experienced in college. Sitting in his hotel room night after night with his evening's cash in front of him, he would get out his list of names, names sent to him by college presidents from across the nation. He would read the reasons why the president thought a particular young person highly deserving and then he would send the money to the one selected. In his personal letter to the lucky one he would make it plain that this money was only a loan, not to be repaid to the donor but to some other deserving person later on when repayment could be made. He wanted to keep the ball rolling on into the indefinite future.

In 1925, in his eighty-second year, Dr. Conwell came to the end of his amazing journey. With his many books written, institutions founded and honors, prizes and medals to his name, he could die content. With thousands of streams of beneficent influence flowing ever outward from the tens of thousands of people he had helped and inspired, he knew that he had indeed chosen "life"; that with the same measure he had used it had been measured to him again.

RIVER OF PEACE

In one of John Greenleaf Whittier's prayer poems he speaks of heaven as a place where "flows forever through heaven's green expansions, *the river of thy peace*." That phrase has been haunting me of late. If ever men have longed for a deep peace that flows along like a river, that time is now. Is it possible?

Look at the chaos and uncertainty on the world stage! Having fought two world wars to attain international peace since the turn of the century, we seem now to be facing a third. Is there any rhyme or reason in all this madness?

Yes, there is. A new world is being born amidst travail and sorrow unparalleled in history because of the vastness of the scale of the operation. The present conflict began in November of 1917 with the Russian revolution which I was privileged to witness. In January of 1918 I was one of two Americans to attend the First Russian Soviet Congress in Leningrad as a spectator. I heard Nicolai Lenin speak for two hours one night. Among other things he said: "Comrades, we have won the revolution in Russia. We shall now proceed to the winning of the revolution throughout the world as we free the peasants and proletariat from slavery. And *if we need to lie and steal and murder* to gain our goal, we shall not hesitate a single moment."

Mr. Lenin was giving expression to the old but false philosophy that "the end justifies the means." The truth is that *the means colors the end*. For thirty-three years I have watched the steady deterioration of the Soviet leadership that is based on that false standard. Communism's goal—the emancipation of the earth's down-trodden millions from poverty and exploitation—is a noble ideal. Revolution was inevitable and the earth's swarming, despairing masses are on the move toward a brighter day. But I am convinced that the deception, brutality and fraud at the heart of political Communism will eventually cause that system of government to die under the impact of outraged humanity. It has always been so and it always will be. It is the verdict of history.

The very trouble that we now face will force the free nations of the earth to strengthen their moral ties in an ever stronger United Nations organization that moves steadily toward some kind of a limited Federal World Government capable of making, interpreting and enforcing world law to prevent war. Its splendid Bill of Human Rights will gradually be implemented and extended until the poorest family on earth will recognize that it has certain inalienable rights that all men are bound to respect. That to me is the meaning of the present chaos and darkness on the world's stage. Reflecting thus, I am able to keep my sanity and my faith in mankind.

But this is not enough. If I am ever to experience peace at the center of life, if I am ever to be buoyed up and carried along by a river of peace comparable to the lovely thing Whittier sings about,

I must come to grips with the forces in my own life that ever tend to destroy that peace.

When Dr. Lucius H. Bugbee was fatally injured a few years ago, his wife and sons wired me to come to Bemus Point, New York, to conduct the memorial service. I had been his Associate Pastor at the Hennepin Avenue Methodist Church in Minneapolis my first four years out of seminary, and I had come to respect and love him above most men I have known.

As I sat alone in his library at Bemus Point before the service, my eye alighted upon Amiel's *Journal*. Instantly I recalled a series of Lenten talks he had given years ago in Hennepin Church based on that century-old journal. I remembered how he had told us of the deep influence this book had had upon his own life and how he had "lived" with it. Reverently I pulled it from the shelf and it fell open at page 98. This remarkable page he had marked. Very slowly I read:

The center of life is neither in thought nor in feeling, nor in will, nor even in consciousness, so far as it thinks, feels, or wishes. For moral truth may have been penetrated and possessed in all these ways, and escape us still. Deeper even than consciousness there is our being itself, our very substance, our nature. Only those truths which have entered into this last region, which have become ourselves, become spontaneous and involuntary, instinctive and unconscious, are really our life—that is to say, something more than our property. So long as we are able to distinguish any space whatever between truth and us we remain outside it. The thought, the feeling, the desire, the consciousness of life, are not yet quite life. But peace and repose can nowhere be found except in life and in eternal life, and the eternal life is the divine life, is God. To become divine is then the aim of life: then only can truth be said to be ours beyond the possibility of loss, because it is no longer outside us, nor even in us, but we are it, and it is we; we ourselves are a truth, a will, a work of God. Liberty has become nature; the creature is one with its creator—one through love. It is what it ought to be; its education is finished, and its final happiness begins. The sun of time declines and the light of eternal blessedness arises.

Our fleshly hearts may call this mysticism. It is the mysticism of Jesus: "I am one with my Father; ye shall be one with me. We will be one with you."

At the bottom of the page he had written, "Thus could Jesus say, 'I *am* the truth.'" And I said to myself, "And thus could Dr. Bugbee also say in a very real sense, 'I *am* the truth.' " The deep meaning of Jesus' words suddenly came alive for me. Jesus lived God's eternal truth so completely that he could truly say, "I *am* the *way*, the *truth* and the *life*"; "I *am* the *resurrection*"; "I *am* the *light* of the world." And he *was*.

But did he not say to his followers, "*Ye are* the light of the world"? Amiel is right. We must not only believe in truth but we must live it moment by moment until there is not even a little space between it and us. Then "we are the truth . . . and the creature is one with the Creator." Said Jesus, "At that day ye shall know that I am in my father, and ye in me and I in you."

I walked over to the window and gazed out across beautiful Lake Chautauqua. "That is why all men trusted Dr. Bugbee so implicitly," I said half aloud. "That is why the young ministers in small, poorly paid charges around Minneapolis called him their true friend and came freely to him, in season and out, to pour out their hearts. He *was* the *truth* to them—and the Father was in him in rich abundance."

But what *is* the truth? How do we recognize it? After all there is quite a difference of opinion among men on that point. First, we must get our central value straight. In the Bureau of Standards in Washington they have weights and measures by which all other weights and measures are judged. Our central measurement in the spiritual realm is the human soul. Whatever tends to enhance, build, integrate and ennoble personality is true and right. Whatever tends to blight or destroy personality is wrong, untrue. First love God and then you can love your neighbor and this is fundamental in Jesus' scale of values.

A state veterinarian, for a consideration, falsely certifies that certain cattle are "free of disease" in order to let them be sold across state lines and thereby endangers the health of many innocent people. Steel company executives whose companies are enjoying the most swollen profits in history, raise the price of steel another five dollars a ton while falsely attributing the increase to "rising costs." By tampering thus with the truth they endanger our whole American way of life by selfishly contributing to the inflation spiral. One church member hears of another church member who holds a different point of view on some doctrinal matter and so, in anger, the first member calls the second brother an "atheist" when he knows it is not true. Thus do God's children, by widening the distance between themselves and truth spread disaster abroad in the land.

Our difficulty is not so much in not knowing what is right. We are bedeviled by our failure to *identify ourselves with the best that we know*. A little lie here, a failure to take our stand there and the gap between ourselves and truth widens and we lose the divine Presence.

I sat down again and reopened Amiel's *Journal* at page 128 and read:

We must learn to look upon life as an apprenticeship to a *progressive renunciation*, a perpetual diminution in our pretensions, our hopes, our powers, and our liberty. The circle grows narrower and narrower; we began with being eager to learn everything, to tame and conquer everything, and in all directions we reach our limit—*non plus ultra*. Fortune, glory, love, power, health, happiness, long life—all these blessings which have been possessed by other men seem at first promised and accessible to us, and then we have to put the dream away from us, to withdraw one personal claim after another, to make ourselves small and humble, to submit to feel ourselves limited, feeble, dependent, ignorant, and poor, and *to throw ourselves upon God for all*, recognizing our own worthlessness, and that we have no right to anything. It is in this nothingness that we recover something of life—the divine spark is there at the bottom of it. Resignation comes to us, and, in believing love, *we reconquer the true greatness*.

Dr. Bugbee had marked that page all up. It was plain to me now. He *was* the truth because he had long ago given up the frantic search for fortune, glory, power and all the trappings of position. In resignation he had become poor and dependent and humble in his utter reliance on God. And in resignation he had reconquered the true greatness. *He had sought first the Kingdom of God and all these things had been added unsought*. High position and considerable power and fame had come to him but they mattered not at all as he weighed them against his Supreme Value—his relationship to the Giver of All. These other things for which men frantically seek and for which they sell their very souls as they play fast and loose with Truth, he held very lightly and evaluated them correctly.

More light on this great man's character was shown by two letters lying on his desk which I was permitted to read. A Methodist minister had written to take violent exception to something Dr. Bugbee had written in *The Sanctuary*—a series of Lenten devotional readings. The brother had completely misinterpreted the author's words and his cantankerous spirit overflowed in a torrent of abuse.

Dr. Bugbee's answer was the last thing he ever wrote. It lay on his desk ready for mailing, an eloquent testimony to the greatness of his heart. Patiently and with the understanding restraint that he always exercised under such provoking circumstances, he had pointed out the minister's error in interpretation and then wished him God's blessing and guidance during the days that lay ahead!

Your job and mine, as I see it, is to come to terms with Truth down deep in the very center of the life of our souls. With Emerson we must discover how to "live in the midst of the traffic of the world with the independence of solitude." Our measuring rod of Truth must come to be the life and insights of Christ himself as we relate this question or that to the enhancement and integration of personality values. Looking steadily at the transparent, radiant, loving Master of Men we shall discover what is the True, the Good and the Beautiful and then we must live it so completely and guilelessly that it becomes indistinguishable from ourselves. In a very real sense we must strive to become "the Way, the Truth and the Life."

They killed Jesus because his deep insights laid bare the deceit and trickery of the orthodox religionists of the day. God did not decree Jesus' death in order that His own anger with sinful men might be appeased by the shedding of His son's blood and thereby put Him in a mood to save lost sinners. Let us be forever done with this artificial, man-made theological insult to a loving God.

Jesus was railroaded to his death on a cross because his transparent goodness and truth-guided life infuriated the deceitful, avaricious, evil churchmen of the day. The shedding of Jesus' blood was *a symbol of life outpoured in love*. When truth is wedded to love through the Divine Presence, it has the power of convicting men of their deceitfulness and sin and of redeeming them. "And I, if I be lifted up (on a cross) will *draw* all men unto me" was Jesus' description of the process.

The deepest tragedy of life happens when men are ensnared in evil's awful net without catching sight of the vision of the uplifted incarnation of Truth in the person of Christ. Then life ends in black futility and hopelessness. Listen to Theodore Dreiser at the close of his career:

"I can make no comment on my work or my life that holds either interest or importance for me. Nor can I imagine any explanation of any life, my own included, that would be either true, or important, if true. Life is to me too much a welter and play on inscrutable forces to permit, in my case, at least, any significant comment. I catch no meaning from all I have seen, and I pass quite as I came, confused and dismayed." There is stark tragedy.

How different were the last days of Jane Addams. When Daniel Poling recalled that she had won the Nobel prize for peace, had greatly reduced juvenile delinquency in Chicago and had opened up at Hull House Settlement new life and opportunity for underprivileged boys and girls, he went to her and asked for the secret of her life. She replied: "I looked up into the face of Christ and then I looked into the faces of those needy boys and girls and *I tried to bring them together.*"

Christ and his Truth, the Good News about God, gave Jane Addams peace and power at the Center of Life. Lacking this, Theodore Dreiser wrote books that said nothing of significance or permanent value to hungry-souled men.

One other thing lay on Dr. Bugbee's desk that showed he shared Jane Addams' optimism about life's final conclusions. I refer to his final words in his published article "After Retirement." "Retirement is not all sunshine," he wrote, ". . . but *we try to make the most of the best and the least of the worst. And when the shadows gather we remember that 'there will be bright skies in the morning.'* "

Bright skies in the morning! Exactly! And a river of peace flowing through our souls straight from the heart of God. I once found myself sitting behind and a little to the side of Jane Addams in a Chicago audience. She had just come from Hull House where she had lived for years surrounded by poverty and disease. Yet, I have never seen anyone on this earth radiate more of the "Peace which passeth understanding." Once, during the meeting, she arose and spoke briefly in answer to a question from the stage. A solemn hush fell over the audience when her name was spoken. She looked up into the face of her Christ very often indeed and then into the faces of needy people and tried to bring them together. In building the True, the Good and the Beautiful into other lives, she found a river of deep peace flowing through her own heart. This resulted in an "emanation of spirit" which any sensitive person could feel even at a distance.

Yes, there can be a river of peace in your heart and mine—and "bright skies in the morning." But an article of such celestial splendor will carry a correspondingly high cost mark. Heaven has no bargain counters where "something else just as good" may be had at a reduced price.

The National Arts Foundation has one hundred and fifty advisory board members composed of leaders from all over the world such as Churchill, Santayana, Olivier, Marian Anderson and Dr. Albert Schweitzer. They were recently asked this question: "Which man today has the best solution for the problems of the world?" First choice was Dr. Albert Schweitzer, of whom they wrote: "He lives only for others. By example he teaches his fellow men to release the forces for good which are in all of us . . . He has a wholehearted respect for all living creatures." Dr. Schweitzer himself wrote: "The greatest man in the world is some unknown person who lives only for others."

Sounds strangely like what an unknown carpenter said in Nazareth nineteen centuries ago. He was the world's greatest expert on the subject of inner peace. And now after the lapse of nearly two thousand years, his most outstanding living disciple is chosen as the man with the best solution to the world's ills. Having reached the pinnacle of success in the fields of philosophy, theology and music, he left it all to study medicine so that he could go to Africa to bring healing and peace to the poorest and most helpless of the sons of men. His strong, rugged face mirrors the peace that he himself has found in serving others. He gives to you and me our one sure clue for finding our own River of Peace.

An old print puts it this way:

I am your friend and my love for you goes deep. There is nothing I can give you which you have not got; but there is much, very much, that, while I cannot give it, you can take. No heaven can come to us unless our hearts find rest in today. Take Heaven! No peace lies in the future which is not hidden in this present little instant. Take Peace. The gloom of the world is but a shadow. Behind it yet within our reach is Joy. There is radiance and glory in the darkness, could we but see and to see we have only to look. I beseech you to look.